Now You Know Me

Seeing the Unhidden Truth
in Settler Colonialism

K'wUNƏMƐN JOE GALLAGHER
AND JOHN MATTERSON

Foreword: Dr. Evan Tlesla Adams

Printed in Korea

Cover & Interior Design: J. Rade & M. Lamont
Front Cover Artwork: Athena Picha & Shane Pointe
PROCEEDING PHOTO: White-faced Scops Owl (Shutterstock)

We acknowledge the support of the Government of Canada through the Canada Book Fund and the
Canada Council for the Arts, and of the Province of British Columbia through the British Columbia
Arts Council and the Book Publishing Tax Credit.

*Hancock House gratefully acknowledges the Halkomelem Speaking
Peoples whose unceded, shared and asserted traditional territories our
offices reside upon.*

Published simultaneously in Canada and the United States by
HANCOCK HOUSE PUBLISHERS LTD.
19313 Zero Avenue, Surrey, B.C. Canada V3Z 9R9
#104-4550 Birch Bay-Lynden Rd, Blaine, WA, U.S.A. 98230-9436
(800) 938-1114 Fax (800) 983-2262
www.hancockhouse.com info@hancockhouse.com

Cover Art by a Coast Salish Uncle and Niece team, Athena Picha and Shane Pointe.

I have taken my knowledge of kʷunəmɛn, Joe Gallagher and combined it with the histories I have heard from many other esteemed persons including John Matterson to create a visual history.

The combined visual elements represent kʷunəmɛn's personal and professional histories, from his Tla'amin family roots as well as his leadership outside of his village.

- The White Owl represents Joe's wisdom and leadership.
- The Quarts Crystal signifies his ability to communicate clearly.
- The North Star his powerful moral compass.
- The Firmament his connection to all that is natural and supernatural.
- The Soccer Ball represents Joe expanding his connection to the broader world including with his friend John who is sharing Joe's history through this book.

Contents

Foreword

Dr. Evan Tlesla Adams
Deputy Chief Medical Officer, First Nations Health Authority,
and Acting Associate Dean Indigenous Health, Simon Fraser
University Medical School

I am honoured to provide the foreword to this history and introduce k'ʷunəmɛn—Joe Gallagher.

Joe and I are both Tla'amin. He is five years older, but we grew up together. I saw him often, as our dads were good friends. They had their differences, but they shared a common work ethic, and both had very high expectations of their children.

Being younger, I looked up to Joe, particularly as a great soccer player, and when he went off to university. He was one of the few people from our community at that time to take that step, which encouraged many others, including me, to follow in his footsteps. In this respect, I am not surprised that he became a strong leader for our people, but I am also in awe of what he has accomplished. I was fortunate to work with Joe as chief medical officer at the First Nations Health Authority.

Joe has suffered a great deal throughout his life. He had no choice but to take the hard road every step of the way, so his ideas are not untested in the real world, as is the case for many other leaders. Though he was one of our best and brightest, he still faced tremendous roadblocks. He is a visionary, and Indigenous and non-Indigenous Canadians alike have benefited from his intellect and hard-won realizations. He imagines Canada in a way that others haven't been able to yet.

As the founding CEO of the First Nations Health Authority, Joe was more than just a change leader. He transformed the way things were done. He would be moving us, his executive team, along and I didn't even realize at the time that he was leading us to do better. He was insistent that we operate using Indigenous practices. He worked with quiet strength but was also impossibly demanding. He would not accept anything done other than properly, even in a health system that is enormous and underachieving. Everyone worked incredibly hard for him. He was able to put solutions in front of all 203 BC chiefs that proved to them that we could achieve better together.

With Joe as a leader, we Indigenous health professionals went from being unnoticed and unimportant to being respected in high-level strategic meetings. We suddenly had seats at the table at the highest level. It was mind-boggling to me that he would just bypass the deans and dozens of health professional committees at a university to get us a seat with the president—and then persuade them to act. We would meet with the heads of health authorities and with ministers and deputy ministers. He got these meetings because he is strategic and convincing, and because his intellect and vision are hard to ignore. He could convince the minister of health, or the head of a hospital, that they were going to work with him to make large-scale changes and commitments.

He could imagine something that none of us could yet see, and he actualized it. He was transforming at an amazing pace. He quietly pushed people to listen and meet their commitments. It was a revelation to watch him ask for, to expect, and even demand that. It's what set him apart. His history is one that needs to be told.

John and Joe's history together and the conversation they bring forward within this book are critical for our times. Allyship is extremely important, and the bar for allies is high. It requires people to willingly engage in a conversation, one that is both egalitarian and sophisticated. People that can consider a Canada where people are all equally important, not just a country that privileges the privileged and divests itself from the marginalized.

After ten years with Joe trying to hire Indigenous people into the First Nations Health Authority, we still had twice as many non-Indigenous as Indigenous employees. There isn't just a place for non-Indigenous people in Indigenous work. There is a need.

Allyship is not just about buying a t-shirt at an Indigenous event or attending a webinar at work and then saying, "Okay, I'm an ally now." It is about changing how you see the entire world and doing the hard work of reconciliation.

It's easy for John and me, or John and Joe, to sit together and break bread, be friends and go to school together. But there is another reality beyond that: the formal contract between the original peoples of this land and settlers who came with the formation of Canada. The dialogue Joe and John are having is exemplary, but unfortunately it is not common.

Their story brings forward a very central concept. It's not about Indigenous people just talking amongst themselves about their place in Canada. It is a story of the need for non-Indigenous people to support a Canada that has Indigenous roots.

Most Canadians hold simplistic notions about their country that remain unchallenged. We need more people to step up and recognize that Canada is not just a country of immigrants, but also that our original inhabitants are an important part of our overall identity—then, now, and in the future. We need a reckoning by Canadians of what we have inherited. Are Canadians simply going to ignore, like previous generations did, an inconvenient truth? Are we going to continue to try to erase what has happened to, for instance, thousands of children?

We need to know where Canada has come from and to know where Canada is going. Now is the time for straight talk, which is what John is working on in his journey with Joe.

This history, through John's voice, also recognizes a very important part of reconciliation. It isn't just Indigenous people who must step up and resolve their challenges. Non-Indigenous people must step up in support of equity, be thankful, and forge a future where Indigenous peoples are clearly seen in their importance to the future of all Canadians.

Introduction: Joe

My name is Joe Gallagher. I am from the Coast Salish Ey7á7juuthem (EYE-a-jooth-um)–speaking people, which includes the ɬaʔəmen (Tla'amin), χʷɛmaɬku (Homalco), λohos (Klahoose), and θaɬaθtuxʷ (K'ómoks) Peoples. These four Peoples were very closely connected, with many family relationships, and have a rich territory in the northernmost part of the overall Coast Salish territory, in what is currently known as southwestern British Columbia. My late mom, Ann, was from the Homalco First Nation, and my late father, Norman, was from the Tla'amin Nation.

Homalco: mid-1900s

Sliammon, mid-1900s. Notice the prominence of the church.

I'm a brother to my older sister, Marina, and my younger brother, Steve. I am a father to my son, Benjamin, and an uncle to Stacia, Corey, Tyler, Jacob, Makeala, Mattias, and Makara (deceased). My siblings and I were born in what settler colonialists called Powell River and raised on the Sliammon Indian Reserve #1. Powell River is a town built on Tla'amin village sites a few kilometers away from where the Tla'amin community is now. Powell River currently has a population of about 13,000 people, while there are now just over 1,100 members of the Tla'amin Nation.

Sliammon was a typical Indian reserve when I was growing up, created by the Indian Act, with a church in the centre. The deliberate genocidal actions of settler colonialism meant the Tla'amin Nation was alienated from its territories, stripped of its culture and language; generations of children were taken to residential school, and the community was left to exist with high unemployment and low levels of education. Alcoholism was prevalent. I grew up in a household where both parents were survivors of residential schools and trying to raise a family in that environment.

Mom's family are from the Homalco First Nation. The Homalco were initially located by white settlers on the reserve known as Church House, which was a small reserve north of Tla'amin at the entrance to Bute Inlet. It was a very isolated community, and its residents have since been relocated to a new reserve in a southern part of their territory, just outside of Campbell River on Vancouver Island. As far back as I can remember, and until recently, my mom's siblings have lived mostly in Vancouver. Now they have returned home to the new reserve.

Dad was from Tla'amin and was raised by his great-grandmother. He spent several years in day schools before spending a year in the residential school in Kamloops. Despite his limited formal education, he was very strong-minded, a hard worker and very entrepreneurial. He was also an elected member of the Indian band council on several occasions.

I began working for my own community to make change, to discover our rich history and teachings and to be part of building a future for the Tla'amin people, for today and future generations. During this time, I had the opportunity to work with Tla'amin leaders in the assertion of our rights and title, which inspired and shaped me into who I am today. During this time, I became a father, with a son for whom I have great hope, and who drives me to shape a better world for him than I experienced, much like my father did for me.

I eventually took on a role of working for all First Nations peoples in what is now known as British Columbia, in support of governance of their own health and wellness. I was working toward a vision that I hoped all "BC First Nations" would be proud of. To achieve this, I have been and am always willing to step into a leadership role and take on the conversation about First Nations rights and title and eliminating Indigenous-specific racism head-on. I know that I am not "less than," and that First Nations and Indigenous peoples are not "less than," as the founding fathers of this country deemed them to be, an idea then perpetuated in Canadian society for over 150 years. Settler colonialism imposed many harms, including oppression and racism, that generated fear and shame for me as a child. That dominated my being then, but this is no longer the case. I had to learn to manage my fears and believe in who I am. Instead, I have committed my life to envisioning a better future for my son, my family, my nation, and all First Nations and Indigenous peoples.

I have grown to come at things from a place of love, compassion, humility, and truth-telling. My hope is for all First Nations and Indigenous people to not feel "less than" or be treated as "less than." We should all know that everything we do and who we are has great value, and that our First Nations worldview and our rights and title are to be recognized and respected in Canadian society. We need recognition that Indigenous peoples are full partners with other Canadians working together to create a truly just society. Recognition that realizes the unique relationship Canada has with the First Nations and all Indigenous peoples of these lands.

Voices in this Book

We have described for you a mountain. We have shown you the path to the top. We call upon you to do the climbing."

—The Honorable Murray Sinclair

Now You Know Me is co-authored, but we made a conscious decision to write it primarily in John's voice as a non-First Nations person. Much of the text written by John is his interpretation of the many discussions we had about Joe's history and Indigenous-specific racism, as well as his own research. It is based on where John is at on his own personal journey toward unlearning and relearning at the time of writing this book. Joe and John realize that this approach will provide content from John's lens that may not be exactly how Joe would articulate it. However, this is a valuable reflection of doing our best to approach this work with humility and a recognition of how much more we all must do to reach shared understandings and eliminate systems of inequity. Where Joe's voice or someone else's is used, it has been noted.

John: This is the story of the learning journey I have undertaken. A journey to see what was already in front of me. My intent is to honour Joe's community, his family, and Joe himself. I am continuing to learn to work against my white-world bias. This publication is a history as I have heard and understand it today.

As a non-First Nations person, I see the need to take responsibility, show humility, open my mind, learn beyond common cultural stereotypes, and move forward in allyship with First Nations.

Notes

Tla'amin Nation is the proper name for the community Joe grew up in. At times we will also refer to it as Sliammon, which is how we knew it, growing up. Tla'amin is First Nations Territory. Sliammon was the name of the reserve set up under the Indian Act.

We use the term "Indian" rather than First Nation often, where it made sense to us historically. No offence is intended.

- We refer to "First Nations and other Indigenous peoples," because in the land known as British Columbia the original Indigenous peoples from the land are First Nations and the only ones with rights and title related to their territory. Other Indigenous peoples who originate from other lands do not have the same rights here.
- This book is the result of an ongoing journey with many lessons still to be learned. We hope that progress has been made between the time of writing and the time of publication.

Trigger Warning. This book deals with topics that may cause trauma for some readers.

Part 1

GETTING TO REALLY KNOW JOE

1. Reacquainted

We arranged to meet in one of the many high-end brew pubs in downtown Vancouver. I arrived early, eager to meet with Joe for the first time in years. This was a few weeks before Covid-19 would change the world, so the pub was packed even though it wasn't yet 5 p.m. Sales reps, stockbrokers, and the like were yelling over each other to get the attention of servers to keep their drinks coming. It was a far cry from the pub in the basement of the University of Victoria student union building where, 40 years earlier, Joe and I drank $1 beers from red solo cups.

The hostess directed me to the only remaining available seats: two stools at a high table against the wall and partially obscured behind a large beam. She tossed a couple of plastic-coated menus on the table, and before she could finish asking, I indicated that I would wait until my guest arrived before ordering a drink. Positioning myself to see around the beam, I watched for Joe to arrive. It didn't register with me at the time that with English Bay prominent in the background, I was on Coast Salish territory.

Eventually I spotted him, looking the same as always, and waved him over. We shared an enthusiastic handshake that included one of those bring-it-in-and-bump-shoulders things that guys do when they are not quite ready to hug. He had arrived a few minutes late. The helicopter returning him to Vancouver from his meeting with the deputy minister of health in Victoria was delayed.

We quickly settled in, enjoying a couple of hamburgers with our beer, reminiscing and talking about our families and careers. The casual setting didn't match the depth of much of our conversation, but the quiet corner we sat in did end up providing some privacy and a buffer from the noise.

Joe k'ʷunəmɛn Gallagher is Coast Salish and grew up in Tla'amin, and I am white and grew up in Powell River on traditional Tla'amin land. We were friends in high school and roommates in first-year university. We lost touch in our early twenties as our lives proceeded in different directions, with each of us becoming deeply rooted in our own ethnicity. I had enjoyed what most would consider a successful career in executive roles for software companies, traveling all over the world, living in white societal norms. Joe was the founding CEO of the First Nations Health Authority, the largest First Nations–owned and –run public service in the country at the time, and was living his identity as a Tla'amin man and deeply involved in nation-building.

Joe spoke that evening with a confidence I had not seen before from my quiet friend. He was still measured but at the same time forthright. We talked about the health work he was doing, and of his personal life. He shared some of the many harms First Nations were still experiencing due to overt racism, systemic racism, and the poor socio-economic conditions resulting from settler colonialism that still exist today. He spoke of working with Knowledge Keepers, and their teachings and traditions. I had never really heard him discuss First Nations issues before, and certainly not with such conviction.

I felt responsible for us not keeping in touch. I had gotten caught up in my career and allowed far too much of my life to be taken over by it. Still, I had thought of Joe often over the years. My mum would share updates on him, mostly from articles in the Powell River newspaper, related to the Tla'amin treaty work he was doing. I haven't been great at staying in touch with any of the people that I went to school with, but in hindsight, when it came to Joe there was more to it than me just being self-absorbed. When he returned to Tla'amin and started working for the community there, I felt he had returned to a world that was inaccessible to me.

That lost connection between our worlds is one reason I was nervous to meet with Joe after more than 30 years. I had looked him up online multiple times over a period of a few months without taking the step of reaching out. I was unsure of the response I might receive. I finally pushed send on an email to the First Nations Health

Authority (FNHA), where he was the CEO. I was pleased to receive his almost immediate response, and we arranged to meet.

Joe spoke of the work he was doing as CEO. Under Joe's leadership of the FNHA, they had built a BC First Nations organization run by First Nations for First Nations. A first of its kind in Canada. His vision was clear. They existed to provide better health and wellness to First Nations and to make decisions for themselves. He was dedicated to making the world a better place. In reflecting on my own career, and on the impact of my work, I realized I had put a lot of effort into making a lot of rich people richer. Joe was making a difference in improving people's health and wellness, and I wanted to be part of something like that.

I asked questions and in a short time recognized just how ignorant I was about so much of his world. I wanted a quick fix: "Tell me what we have to do." But there is no simple solution.

I had come to dinner hoping to rediscover some of myself through a connection to an old friend, and the evening was more than living up to that expectation. I didn't want it to end. I asked Joe if he would like another beer. He politely declined. He couldn't afford to be even a little impaired in public. I could have stumbled out of the pub after a couple more drinks and no one would think much about it, other than that I had had a good time. As a First Nations man, and one with a prominent position, Joe is held to a different standard.

I left dinner with many questions on my mind beyond my need for personal rediscovery. How did we, as a society, get to this point in our treatment of First Nations, and how did Joe become so successful, given all the roadblocks he has had to overcome?

While that dinner was a tipping point for me committing to learning the truth and advocating for First Nations, it was not a full-on *aha* moment. I had a long journey ahead. I still do.

2. A Change in My World

It was a major change in my health that led me, or more accurately pulled me, to finally reconnect with Joe.

In 2014, I developed frozen shoulder and a slight limp. After researching frozen shoulder, I was able to explain it away as one of those things that can just happen. Plenty of people I spoke with knew of someone who had had it. Limping was not new to me. I had been dealing with knee injuries from playing soccer for years. It was harder to explain away the challenges I started having trouble forming even the most basic chords on a guitar, but it wasn't as if I was that great to start with. Next up, I was struggling to carve our Christmas turkey, and my brother asked me if I was drunk. I wasn't. A month later, I was starting to experience small tremors in my left hand and leg. I chose to ignore all these less-than-subtle hints. Fortunately, I had a great family doctor and access to some of the best healthcare in the world.

In February 2015, I had an appointment for a routine annual physical. It was only a few minutes into his examination that my doctor declared I had Parkinson's. He would send me to a neurologist to confirm, but he was certain. I went immediately into denial. I told him I was only shaking because it was cold in the examining room. It didn't take long for my denial to dissipate.

My world perspective changed that day. I was able to function at work as I normally had for two more years by taking on a job that required less travel, but as I reached the end of 2017, I had to accept that I couldn't continue working. That transition was difficult. For all my adult life, my job had defined me. Then, in an instant, when someone would ask me what I did, I no longer had an answer. I would stumble over my words, talking about what I used to be. This started me on a search for a new identity. Reconnecting with Joe gave me an opportunity to open my mind as I never had before.

Through my journey to redefine myself, I would come to see that my search for an identity was minor relative to Joe's. He has spent most of his life in search of his.

3. Contrasting Worlds

Joe: *"Everything just seemed not good enough, and no matter what I did, I was still brown, I was an "Indian," and everywhere in Canada, institutions and people would not let me forget that. It can get so bad that you learn to not like the color of your own skin!"*

John: On the surface, our lives looked much the same when we were kids. We grew up in the same small town, played on the same soccer teams, and not only went to the same school but were in most of the same classes. I didn't comprehend the size of the socio-economic gap that existed between our lives until we started this journey. All these years later, I also now understand that soccer was much more than just a game for Joe. It was a major component in establishing his identity. Being great soccer players was one of the things people in Tla'amin were allowed to be proud of.

Joe used the term "you know" a lot when he was explaining his history to me. I have edited that out of our discussions, but the reality is, a lot of the time I just didn't know. We lived similar lives, but that changed when we went home at the end of each day.

Joe and I first met when we were 13 and we became good friends. We talked a lot as teenagers, but we never got into great depth. Unlike all the white friends I grew up with, Joe was not a regular in our home. I don't remember there being any hesitation on my part. There was certainly nothing conscious. Joe has since told me that he wouldn't have felt comfortable walking alone in my neighborhood, which surprised me. Grief Point, where I grew up, was perhaps Powell River's most affluent neighborhood.

I never went inside Joe's home in Tla'amin. I drove to pick him up a few times. I saw the broken-down cars and poor housing on the reserve, and I felt like I was being watched as I drove along the gravel road on the waterfront toward Joe's house in my dad's bright red Volkswagen Bug. I was certain I was somewhere I didn't belong and wasn't welcome. I didn't talk to Joe about it at the time.

Joe's childhood home. The garage at the back includes Joe's first consulting office.

John's childhood home

Joe as a boy

John as a boy

Looking back, I see now that our different environments had a huge impact on us as kids and how we saw the future. Joe grew up with a ceiling he needed to try to reach for. The privilege I grew up with provided endless opportunity. One of us was striving to be like our parents, while the other was struggling not to. At that age, I didn't see beyond my own world.

Regardless of our differences, we were friends, and when we graduated from high school, we made plans to go to UVic as roommates. When we got to university, and out of Tla'amin and Powell River, I didn't comprehend what Joe was experiencing.

As a roommate, Joe would say to me that he wanted to find a way to make things better for his people. I suppose at that time I thought I knew what he meant, but only because we didn't get into a lot of detail. Whatever his specific intentions were at the time, he most certainly has made things better. I enjoyed being his roommate. The only downside for me of living with Joe was a lot of wet, smelly soccer socks.

Our friendship grew to the point that he was the best man at my first wedding. (I married young.) Shortly after this, I moved from Victoria to Vancouver, became too involved in my career, and lost touch with many friends, including Joe.

I grew up on the traditional territory of the Tla'amin Nation in Powell River, BC. My mum, Kathleen, and dad, Dal, arrived in Powell River after they were married in 1956. Dad grew up in the BC communities of Ucluelet and Ladner. Mum arrived in Vancouver from England as a teenager.

I grew up in a supportive and nurturing home. For those of you old enough to remember TV from the 1960s, there was a *Leave it to Beaver* familiarity to the way I was raised. My parents were a consistent presence for my three brothers and me, and they were interested in what we had to say. Our family sat together for dinner each night. I learned more at that table than I ever did in school.

I always felt safe. It's not that I never worried about anything or had no frustrations, but I have never experienced physical or mental abuse. While our parents offered support, they were never over the top. They led by example. We didn't get too full of ourselves.

I focused on soccer, but my brothers and I loved all sports. We were always out playing with our friends somewhere. We rode our bikes and organized road hockey or baseball games depending on the season. We played in our yard and shot hoops against the net at the side of the house.

I grew up comprehending on some level that I was lucky, but I had no idea what that really meant. As a white, straight, able-bodied male, I was as privileged as one could get. I've had, and still have, every advantage. I just did not recognize the extent of that before starting on this journey with Joe.

In contrast, the memories that Joe has of his childhood and teen years are not happy ones. He was born into a world defined by fear and shame that seemed to be everywhere. From Joe's view, it originated with a volatile home life dominated by his father, Norman's, temper and alcohol abuse.

Although his parents both worked hard to provide the best home and quality of life for them, Joe's memories are flooded with dark times. He felt alone, with no place to go. Afraid of the next incident of violence or abuse and at times numb to it all. As a child, he was good at school, but still that was never good enough to satisfy Norman. It seemed Norman was always angry, and when he wasn't, he was on the verge. Joe didn't understand his anger then, but he has a much better understanding of his context now. Joe even sometimes shares the anger, but he expresses it in a much different way.

Norman's personality and mood set the tone in his family. They would quietly sit down and have dinner together. Any conversation depended on Norman's mood. His temperament influenced everything. Joe's approach was to avoid getting him riled up. Life was easier that way. There was a lot of sitting quietly. No open discussion or debate. When Norman talked, it was the time for him to tell them what he thought. When Norman wasn't around, his mom, Ann, would talk a lot more. It was like two different worlds for Joe and his siblings.

Violence and abuse were always close at home on the reserve, and racism was always there in town. As for sports, Joe didn't shine much when he was young, and he certainly was not good enough to meet Norman's expectations. Driving Joe home from a game when he was a young teenager, Norman was less than subtle in telling him to quit soccer. Joe was "too f'ing slow." Norman made it clear that Joe was a disappointment to him. There was Joe, a young boy falling short of his dad's expectations, and to make matters worse he had no grandparents—all in a world that didn't accept him for who he was or who he was trying to be.

4. Starting the Journey

Joe: *John's and my life represent a human history of two journeys that had an intersection early on, in a context where we were friends as teenagers, but being worlds apart without really knowing why. We went our separate ways for about 30 years, living our lives; there was a tremendous amount of individual growth for both of us. Recently our journeys have intersected once again, and we have rekindled our friendship, with a deeper appreciation for life and a common desire to continue to make a positive impact for our children and the world around us. All the things we have done and experienced have contributed to the richness of our friendship and the ability to talk about something important, most of which was unspoken when we were younger.*

We use the word history *rather than* story. *Knowledge Keeper Sulksun explains that we are not telling a* story. *This is the truth. This is not made up. Too often, on our journey to fight for our rights and title, lawyers would tell a judge that we were just telling stories, implying they were not facts and that we as a people/nation don't exist. We are telling* history. *These are facts and our truths as we know them.*

In talking with John and telling my history, I have had to go back to some very difficult times and relive the pain of experiences. Other members of my family or my community may recall things differently, but this is my truth and how I experienced things, and I am not intending to take away from theirs. I am still working through memories that are suppressed because of trauma. I do know with certainty that there were periods in my life when I spent too much energy navigating through the negative and not enough time living life and celebrating.

From my point of view, whether I live in the Tla'amin community or in Vancouver, I continue to navigate the system around me to live my best life. Vancouver, and many other places in Canada, have become multicultural, and the conversation around social justice is more important than ever. As that conversation evolves, we can't ignore the unique situation of Indigenous people in Canada and our history of settler colonialism.

When John and I talk together about these issues, we can think about the future, when our grandchildren meet, and ask ourselves: What will they talk about? We have an opportunity to set some of that agenda. We can work together to change the narrative moving forward, towards a vision for a better future. If we are proactive, we can work together to shape the path forward.

Proactive listening, learning, and understanding only works as a mutual process. I appreciate our conversations and John's willingness to bring his humility and be open to hearing points that are difficult for him, in learning about my truths and the truths of our shared history. For myself, I try to do the same. I remember John, while we were teenagers, as a good friend. He was considerate, ambitious, and could be opinionated and pointed. Today I know him as someone with the maturity of his life experiences that fuel his sense of purpose and compassion to make the world a better place. I have so much I still need to know about John and his life to understand how he got to where he is today.

Our history is a narrative we need in society today. As a First Nations leader, in the roles I have had and the life that I have lived, you see me dealing with difficult issues. You see me evolving, you see me changing, and then you see me trying to make change. I work extremely hard at this, but I know I can't make change by myself. I don't hold the power and privilege to make this change. So, many others who do have power and privilege need to do their part, too. John reached out to me, and we had this opportunity to reconnect as friends. Now we are partnered in this project and for the first time truly working towards a meaningful and common goal.

John: Soon after reconnecting, in June 2019, I learned that Joe was receiving an honorary Doctor of Laws degree from the University of Victoria. Watching the ceremony live online, I became overwhelmed with emotion. Watching convocation ceremonies has that effect. Seeing Joe wearing Tla'amin regalia—a cedar hat—was a first for me. His words were both humble and wise, but I was taken in most by the gentle confidence he carried on the stage.

The university was recognizing him for work he did for First Nations rights and self-determination. For advances in a vision of health and wellness. For leadership in the building of the FNHA, driven by First Nations perspectives on health and wellness, and in getting a commitment to cultural safety and humility from BC Health. For his role as chief negotiator for the Tla'amin Nation, and for being a University of Victoria alumnus and soccer player.

I was proud to know the man he had become, how committed he was to his cause, and all that Joe has accomplished as a First Nations man. He rose to become a highly respected and accomplished soccer player, and CEO of the First Nations Health Authority. A feat Ian Potter, former federal assistant deputy minister of First Nations and Inuit Health, described to me as "the most radical, innovative and positive thing that has happened in First Nations health care in over 100 years."

We started scheduling regular calls, which began a mutual learning journey for Joe and me. I was learning from Joe in a *Tuesdays With Morrie* kind of way, while he was also on a learning journey, discovering more of his own history and gaining a better understanding of his own identity. Thanks to Covid-19, we quickly became adept at using Zoom.

We spent hours together, with Joe sharing his history and me listening and learning. A challenging experience for me at times, having always been a talker. We shared laughs, but most of our conversations were serious. I would leave each call more inspired but also feeling a lot of pain from Joe. Some of Joe's history of physical abuse, alcohol and racism have been included in this book, but there is much more that we chose to omit.

Joe frequently became emotional as he talked about feeling alone, growing up. He felt different from everyone else, including his peers in Tla'amin. He was good at school but not able to keep up in sports. They were drinking, and he wasn't. They were learning the Ayajuthum language, and he wasn't. He was bullied, and as the oldest boy he felt the need to protect his family from his dad. He had no grandparents around to learn from.

During our discussions, Joe was both persuasive and patient. As he has done in his work, he allowed me to learn rather than try to sell me on ideas, but he was also very determined that I grasp the truth. He allowed me to stumble through conversations about racism and privilege as I gained an understanding of my own truths. As an example, he never called me a racist. I think the closest he got was to call me "insensitive at times." We would shift the conversation to something that wasn't necessarily about racism, and then suddenly I would say to him, as the pieces of the puzzle came together in my head, "I am a racist." We had deep conversations about hereditary chiefs versus elected chiefs, and regarding pipelines. I never felt like I needed to agree with him. There was no selling of ideas going on. We were collaborating.

I felt guilty as he and I talked more and more. So many issues I wished I had understood and been supportive of long before. Not just from the shame of the residential schools, or the Sixties Scoop and everything else connected with colonialization, but because I was so blind to what was and is still happening right in front of me. I consider myself well-informed and educated, yet I was ignorant of so much. Why have so many of us ignored the treatment of First Nations people? In Canada it is our shame, yet most of us don't acknowledge it or perhaps even know much about it. With Joe's help, I began opening my mind to the many things our schoolbooks missed, and to the misconceptions I held.

Joe recommended I read Rupert Ross's book *Indigenous Healing— Exploring Traditional Paths*[1], which was an ideal place to start my journey. I was also invited to hear Rupert speak. He is the author

---

1   Ross, Rupert. *Indigenous Healing—Exploring Traditional Paths.* Penguin Canada. Kindle Edition.

of three books related to his experiences working with Indigenous people. He is a white former Crown prosecutor from Northern Ontario who has been on a long journey to understand the impact of settler colonialism. His humble story examines the impact of residential schools and other destructive forces. He describes his experience getting to understand a world where Indigenous people see a natural order that starts with the land, then the plants, then the animals and finally the people. He sees the potential for a future of Indigenous wellness that will have a positive impact on First Nations as well as the rest of the Canadian population.

I needed to learn more. It was the start of an emotional journey for me that had Joe's full support. Not comparable to what First Nations people face day after day, but emotional, nonetheless. I was starting to recognize my part in settler colonialism and acknowledge my bias. It didn't take much time for me to recognize that Joe grew up oppressed, but it took much longer for me to see what appears so obvious to me now. I grew up privileged. I have received unearned advantage all my life, while Joe, and other First Nations people that lived so close to me, have received unearned disadvantage all their lives.

Our journey has provided me with a deeper understanding of the meaning of Truth and Reconciliation. Truth is understanding the conditions under which First Nations people live today caused by harmful white settler dominance: their poor health, housing, and infrastructure. It is also about understanding and acknowledging their history, their rights, and the brutal theft of their way of life by white settlers.

I grew up thinking the "Indian" problem was one they simply needed to step up and fix themselves. That they just needed to get over their past and move on by getting jobs and stopping their drinking. I didn't comprehend the long-term oppression under which they were living, because I didn't understand the impact those of us with privilege had, and still have, on First Nations.

5. My White Lens

Joe: *Each of us can see things through our own eyes, but I have spent my entire life being forced to see things from the eyes of people like John, and John is finally now working to see things through mine. It's the strength of our friendship and the journey that we've both been on and how it came back together that has created an environment founded in humility and respect, where we trust one another enough to be vulnerable and to go on this journey together.*

Over the years, in my career and in life, I have met many people, both First Nations and non–First Nations, who have been great partners. Not just through the easy projects or initiatives, but the tough ones, too. My interest is to try to see how First Nations and Indigenous peoples can be part of and thrive in any environment they choose. Not just succeeding in whatever professions they chose, but being successful, being true to themselves, and being at their best. For a First Nations person, this means supporting him or her in their authentic identity as a First Nations leader, an identity that flows from who they are, and accepting them as a leader in mainstream systems, a leader who brings new value to the conversation based on our teachings, values, and philosophies.

The debates that John and I get into around contentious issues like pipelines will not work if we are disrespecting one another and not accepting each other's worldviews, or specifically recognizing that it has been the First Nations view of rights and title that is legitimate but has been historically ignored, and that has led to conflict. I can appreciate the challenge this is for John, who is just learning about my history and First Nations worldviews, while I have spent my entire life navigating his worldview. That is what we are exploring. Becoming great partners, trying to build a bridge to the future.

There is an opportunity to build new relationships between settler Canadians and the first inhabitants of these lands and waters. If we do that with respect, humility, and integrity, we have a chance of working through tough issues. If you don't have a good relationship, people end up drawing lines in the sand and disrespecting one another.

John: Powell River's population, when I was growing up, was almost entirely white. Tla'amin reserve land, or Sliammon as we called it then, is north of Powell River, and when I was young, I had no interaction with the people there. My knowledge of "Indians" came from TV and movies. I didn't relate those Indians to people in Tla'amin—they didn't look or dress the same. The reserve was a place we would drive through occasionally. We never stopped.

In the summer before the start of junior high, I was with a group of boys from my neighborhood playing pickup baseball. Hanging around afterward, some of the older kids were telling us about the Indian bullies we would have to face when we got to Brooks Junior High the following September. I am sure they used a more derogatory term than "Indian." The story was that these Indian kids would always sit on opposite sides of the main school hallway with their legs sticking out and try to trip you as you walked by. That was enough to scare this baby-faced, skinny, blond 13-year-old, but the story continued. If they got you to the ground, they would stick you with needles.

Despite my almost nonexistent First Nations exposure, I was frightened of the "Indians" I would meet in junior high. As it turned out, some of the Indian kids did sit in one of the hallways I walked down every day, but it is only in looking back now that I recognize I was never actually bullied, nor did I witness others being bullied. One of my many embedded misconceptions.

As I got older, I continued to live life protected within my white privilege, despite all my global travels. While I did witness extreme poverty in many places, I always returned at the end of the day to four- and five-star hotels.

After living in and around Vancouver until I was 40, I moved to Ann Arbor, Michigan. Ann Arbor had a 71 percent white population, compared to close-by Detroit at 15 percent white. From Michigan, my job moved to Redwood City, California. We bought a home in neighboring San Carlos, which was 75 percent white, versus Redwood City at 43 percent. In both cases, we moved where we were told the schools were better and safer. I knew what this was code for, but I didn't admit it even to myself. Polite white people didn't talk about race.

Even when we moved to Singapore, we lived in a huge condominium complex that was predominately white. This was primarily because the government separated us from the locals, but we were still located in one of the most coveted parts of Singapore. We also knew that the very strict laws in Singapore applied more to some races than others.

We now live in Tsawwassen, BC, which, while being on the traditional territory of the Tsawwassen First Nation, is not part of their modern treaty land. The town of Tsawwassen is one of the whitest communities in the Vancouver area.

Up until very recently, Joe was the only non-white friend I had.

Looking back, I have seen a lot of the world, but all through a white lens. I now recognize that, while the people of Tla'amin were not invisible to me, I did shamefully view them collectively as "less than."

When I was 15, three friends and I managed to get our hands on a 26-ounce bottle of Bacardi rum. We were in the basement of my home, playing pool, while my little brother was asleep upstairs. My parents were expected home at 9 p.m., and the plan was we would go somewhere else at that point and drink it. Then, someone came up with the brilliant idea that we could have just one sip, which led to another, which led to my parents arriving home to see two of my friends running away by scrambling over the back fence, another surrendering, while I was passed out on a La-Z-Boy in the living room with Supertramp playing at full volume on the stereo. Not my finest moment.

The following morning, my dad was very insistent that I tell him where the rum came from. I don't remember anymore. I suspect it was supplied by someone's older sibling, but there was no way I was going to tell my dad who it was. When he insisted, I told him that "some Indian guy" had bootlegged for us. I don't think he really believed me, but it was a plausible story.

That I was able to come up with the response I did so quickly while in a fog illustrates just how we thought about First Nations people back then. When my dad asked me who specifically it was, I said I didn't know. Having spent all my life in Powell River, I knew almost everyone, but I was much less likely to know someone from Tla'amin. Joe and I were friends at the time. I didn't tell him the end part of this story until we started this journey together.

The people in Tla'amin were much less visible to the people of Powell River. They had been physically moved out and segregated to create space for white settlers. We didn't use racial slurs or openly criticize anyone from Tla'amin in our home, but others did. We were taught to respect everyone, but the community looked down on the people of Tla'amin. Being part of the community, it affected all of us. It is going to take generations to recover from this if we don't face racism and ignorance proactively. We must become allies. Today, I too am standing up and saying: *"Less Than, No More."*

6. Racism and White Privilege

Joe: *When I was young, all I used to think of was how dark the world was. There were so many things happening that I wanted to stop, but as a child had no power to change it. I knew I didn't want dysfunction or alcoholism in my life. I was clear on what I didn't want. That was the only reference point I had at the time. Over the years, I have embraced the Serenity Prayer, and I acknowledge that I grew up in a family and on an "Indian Reserve" where alcoholism was prevalent, among so many other factors I would learn to understand as time went by. With all that, one thing was certain: I did not want to raise my son in an environment where he would be subjected to the dysfunction I experienced. I had to break the cycle.*

Like too many other First Nations people, I have struggled to overcome fear and shame, to not let them get the best of me. I had to find a way to survive the violence and abuses brought on through alcoholism, oppression, and racism. Life on the reserve was tough. I was picked on by rez kids for being too good at school. Called an "egghead" or a "nerd" and bullied for not being strong enough. I just tried to keep everything calm in my life, including my household, as best I could, but to no avail. On top of all that, as an "Indian" I had to deal with being treated as "less than" by white society in everything I did. At school, sports, walking in stores or in white neighbourhoods, I was made to feel I didn't belong. Officially I was born a "ward" of the federal government. I didn't know how to take it all.

John: I came to the discussion ignorant of a lot of what Joe has told me, but it's not like I was totally in the dark. I had years of life experiences to call on to help me be open to what I had previously been blind to.

In traveling the world, I have been welcomed into people's homes on six continents. I came to recognize that at the most basic of levels, we all just want what's best for our families. I enjoyed learning new traditions in places I visited. I also recognized plenty of inequity. Yet, despite having grown up in Powell River on the traditional territory of Tla'amin, like too many Canadians, I was ignorant and/or simply chose not to see First Nations.

Before Joe and I started our journey, I saw myself as a kind person. Now I recognize I am racist, white-privileged, complicit in socialized superiority ... and yes, I am still a kind person.

When we were young friends, I knew Joe was an "Indian," of course, but I saw him as more like me, or at least, in my lack of humility, I assumed he wanted to be more like me. I didn't comprehend the extent of my unearned advantage back then.

Why wouldn't he want to have my life rather than live on the reserve, which in my view had a lower standard of living? I lacked any depth of understanding, but I knew the Tla'amin community had dysfunction. I only considered his situation in terms of my world, never his.

I never intentionally tried to hurt Joe; he was my friend. But I know now that some of my words and actions came out that way. We went to a Halloween party just two months after arriving at UVic, as the Lone Ranger and Tonto (I was Tonto). Seems so bad now, but at the time I thought it was clever. I believed that what I was doing was showing how open I was. I thought I was showing that I wasn't a racist.

Joe: *We didn't know better. I was trying to fit in. I think back to me leaving home and the state of First Nations racism at the time. I was impacted by so many things that forced me not to like myself as an "Indian." I thought, okay, sure, I'll be a good guy for once. I'll be the Lone Ranger. I'll be the hero rather than the sidekick. Of course, I also knew this was a false narrative. Wearing a cowboy hat couldn't change the colour of my skin. I was trying to fit in to a world where no one looked like me. Now that I am older, of course, I understand how screwed up that was.*

John: In our second year in Victoria, I had moved into a basement suite with my girlfriend, and Joe's brother had come to live with him off-campus. I wasn't playing soccer on a team at that time, but Joe and I still spent a lot of time together kicking a ball around. One day I was with him at the soccer field next to the apartment they were living in. Back in those days, I seldom stopped talking. There I was with Joe, his brother and two girls about our age from Tla'amin, and I started into my usual banter. I received a glaring stare from one of the girls. I didn't even know what I had said, but it was clear that it wasn't appreciated. I was quiet for the rest of our time together. I was in Joe's other world for that brief period. It is one of those moments I wish I could have back. I would like to have tried to have a discussion to understand the situation. I just wasn't mature enough back then. I wasn't ready to get comfortable with getting uncomfortable.

When you have a life of privilege, you don't necessarily know you have it. It's like riding a bicycle with the wind always at your back. You simply learn to think you are better than you are.

I have never been afraid to call 911, or afraid of the police. I have always been treated extremely well in the medical system. I trust the legal system to treat me fairly. I've never had trouble getting a job, and I have never had to turn the other cheek when being insulted by my friends about my race.

I did struggle initially while Joe and I discussed the topics of racism, white privilege, white fragility, and white supremacy. I was uncomfortable both with the terms and in understanding how they could apply to me. We discussed these topics repeatedly. I asked a lot of questions, and I did a lot of my own reading and reflection. If we are to truly reconcile, we need to be willing to talk about things even if they make us vulnerable.

I have participated in white solidarity, meaning I have seen or heard incidents of racism, thought it was wrong, but have remained silent at work, silent in sports, and silent with friends, rather than speaking up where I should have. I have laughed and told "jokes" I shouldn't have told.

It is difficult. Perhaps we don't want to call out a racist "joke" for fear of not fitting in, being told to "lighten up" or "it's just a joke," concerned that we will lose some of our unearned advantage by being pushed out of our privileged group. Even if it is difficult, we need to learn to speak up. If we remain silent, we are only adding fuel to the issue.

Joe uses a canoe analogy to explain this kind of learning journey. When you first get into a canoe, you learn the basics while in calm water. At the start, while practicing simple strokes, it can become easy to think you are ready for more when you are not. You may also tend to get comfortable in the calm water and not venture further, but that won't get you to the other side. As you progress, you may find yourself in rough waters and need to return to shore and rethink your situation. You then need to return to the canoe and keep challenging your limits. It is something that requires practice and commitment.

Gaining an understanding of my own racism was an important step. The next was recognizing that the First Nations experience is unique compared to groups that have immigrated to Canada. While they may share some similar experiences, First Nations also are dealing with socio-economic inequities whose origins go back to the very founding of Canada, built on a foundation of male white supremacy. Canada was established, at its core, with a colonial blueprint of getting rid of First Nations. First Nations living under the Indian Act, unlike all other Canadians, to this day remain wards of the federal government.

The emotion that goes into my conversations with Joe is deep. This never turns off for Joe. The need for him to carry such a burden is incredibly unfair and unhealthy. Our journey is far from over. I continue to learn of the resilience of a people that survived every attempt to get rid of them by white settler colonizers. There is so much we can learn from First Nations about spirituality, sharing, and sustainable practices.

The start of my journey required recognizing and understanding my white-world bias. It is a difficult task to move away from feeling comfort about the way things are. I didn't realize how much of an impact the journey of telling the story would have on the two of us. So much anger, sadness, and loss that needed to be expressed.

Joe and I went from our teenage relationship, where we enjoyed each other's company and the unspoken parts were "just the way things are," to an adult relationship where we are acknowledging that those ways weren't good.

7. Embracing our Shame

John: Canada was established through pervasive racialization of First Nations peoples by the state, as determined by patriarchal, white supremacist, Christian beliefs and values. This is captured in the painting *The Fathers of Confederation* by Robert Harris. This familiar painting was commissioned by the Canadian government in 1883. The original painting, capturing the historic gathering of those setting out plans for Confederation, was destroyed in a fire at the Parliament Buildings in 1916. In 1967, Rex Woods was commissioned to recreate the painting as part of the 1967 Centennial celebrations. He added more stodgy white men. This is clearly an origin story that many Canadians are proud of. It also provides a reminder of the exclusion of First Nations peoples.

As we expose more of our history, many Canadians are now acknowledging the horrible events of our past. Many of us feel shame at the atrocities committed by those who came before us, but many are also quick to say it had nothing to do with them. They deny any accountability for actions taken by Canadians who came before us.

I am a proud Canadian. I am proud of Terry Fox. I am proud of Michael J. Fox, Dr. Peter Bryce and Dr. Roberta Bondar. I was proud when Canada's women's and men's teams both won gold in Olympic hockey in 2010. I proudly tell my American friends that it was Canadian Alexander Graham Bell who invented the telephone in 1876, and Canadian James Naismith who originated the game of basketball in 1891. I am proud of all the individual Canadians that have made Canada a better place and have pushed for racial, gender, and LGBTQ rights. I am proud of all those who have driven positive change, making Canada a place where people from all over the world want to live. These points of pride have nothing to do with anything I personally did, but I am still proud of them.

I am also not directly responsible for First Nations being robbed of their rich way of life. For causing their starvation, stealing their land, and forcing them to live on reserves while settlers profited off their land. I did not personally cause their poverty, shorter life expectancy, higher incarceration rates, or higher suicide rates. But these are all realities in Tla'amin, British Columbia, and Canada as a whole. I did not do these things, but like the pride I have in things I didn't do as a Canadian, I also own the shame. We need to stop conveniently saying the past has nothing to do with us.

It's not that we need to live in constant guilt about the past. Canada has a history of supporting those less fortunate than us. Together, if we learn and acknowledge the truth, we can rise and commit ourselves to reconciliation in a way we can all be proud of.

When I discussed the example of Team Canada winning hockey gold in 2010 as one of the Canadian accomplishments I was proud of, Joe didn't respond as I would have expected. He didn't share the joy in a game that was watched by 80 percent of Canadians. The difference in this case is that Joe cared about hockey, just not Team Canada. He is still a Leafs fan today (even Joe isn't perfect), because when we were young, George Armstrong was their captain and a great player. He was also a proud First Nations person. An Anishinaabe.

It wasn't that he was cheering against Canada, but he found it difficult to support a team whose country continues to treat First Nations the way we do. While I was initially surprised that he didn't care about this game, it was also a powerful indicator of how deep the pain goes for Joe and other First Nations people. I aspire to get to a place where Joe can feel good about being Canadian.

Part 2

WHITE SETTLERS – A DESTRUCTIVE PATH

8. Ignoring First Nations History

Joe: *"Less Than, No More" refers to a frame of mind that is against inequity. It's a statement for truth and justice for all First Nations and Indigenous peoples. It is a statement for non-First Nations/ Indigenous settlers to see us for who we are, our rights and title, our culture, language, and ceremonies, our families and societies—and fully realize that we are not "less than," as Canadian white supremacy has falsely deemed us to be, for its own purposes. We are the original landowners and peoples of these lands.*

John: Because so much of the suffering Joe experienced growing up on the reserve was the result of the Canadian government trying to "get rid of the Indian problem," we need to look back before we move forward.

Most of the research I have done for this book has come from hours of time with Joe, other First Nations individuals, and leaders from the health community and government. I have also gained a perspective from discussions with my predominantly white friends. One could argue that talking over beer following a round of golf hardly qualifies as research, but many of those discussions with people of privilege were both insightful and uncomfortable. Some individuals were supportive, but these talks also exposed a high level of ignorance and white fragility. I was told recently, for example, that I should be careful not to drink too much of the Kool-Aid.

You see, as a North American white male with British ancestry, the less you know about your history, the better you are going to feel about it. It may feel more comfortable to live in the past. We may fear the future, but we need to search for the truth.

Most of my friends and I grew up in a time where much of the world map was still pink, recognizing all the British colonies. We saw "leadership" of a quarter of the world's population as a point of pride. After carrying that belief for decades, many find it difficult to finally wake up and accept how the First Peoples in these colonies were treated. White people have been responsible for great innovations and scientific development. We have also been responsible for putting ourselves above others in the world, and of imposing our way for personal advantage.

Most of us didn't learn in school about, or get a good grasp of, the interdependency European settlers had with First Nations people throughout most of the fur trade era. We weren't taught the positive role First Nations people played in helping settlers when they arrived in what became Canada, only to have their kindness countered by having their entire way of life stripped from them.

White settlers have failed to acknowledge the extent of deliberate, racially motivated and ongoing attempts to impose laws, restrict practices and separate families, all with the stated intent by the government to "kill the Indian."

As I share what I am learning on my journey, I hear what I like to call "yeah-buts." I had a white friend tell me, while on the topic of First Nations, that he thought there was no country in the world less racist than Canada. He may be right. We are open to immigration and are proud that people see Canada as a safe, good place to come to. We are happy that we can provide the opportunity for a better life.

But let's look at that another way—from a First Nations perspective. Imagine your community was facing high rates of suicide, your people were dying in hospitals waiting for treatment, they were being incarcerated at rates higher than others, and you didn't have access to clean drinking water. Would you say, oh that's okay, at least we are lucky to live in Canada?

The United Nations Human Development Index[2] ranks countries based on life expectancy, education, and income. In 2016, Canada was ranked 12th out of 189 countries. The Canadian government did further

2   Application of the United Nations Human Development Index to Registered
      Indians in Canada 2006-2016 Indigenous Services Canada > Research and
      Statistics – https://www.sac-isc.gc.ca/eng/1579883155069/1607442298277

analysis that concluded that Registered[3] "Indians" in Canada would rank 52nd, and those living on a reserve would rank 78th. Obviously, this is a long way from equity.

Our multicultural environment is lauded around the world in rankings that often only describe Canada's negative relationship with First Nations in some limited sort of footnote. First Nations are not the same as other groups. They are the original inhabitants of our land. They have rights that have been ignored, they are victims of genocide, and they have been pushed into a sometimes consciously, sometimes unconsciously, biased void by most Canadians. Is it really okay for me to just continue to drive through Tla'amin and pretend that the poverty I see has nothing to do with me?

I suspect that for some non–First Nations readers, the statements above may sound too harsh, or perhaps you don't think they apply to you. That is "white fragility." I ask you to look at the situation from the viewpoint of First Nations people and keep that in mind as you read forward.

---

3   Under the Indian Act, the Government of Canada claims the authority to decide who is and is not an "Indian." The law has mechanisms in place that decrease the number of Status Indians over time. It is still in effect, even though it does not uphold UNDRIP, which affirms the right of Indigenous people to decide for themselves who is a member of their community.

9. This Land is My Land

This is not a book on Canadian history, but to understand Joe's experiences, we must become more aware of the deep historical roots that were disrupted or destroyed by the arrival of white settlers.

There were many actions taken by white settlers that robbed First Nations of their way of life in a very short period. The arrival of smallpox, the Catholic Church, and alcohol all directly affected the world Joe grew up in. White settlement of significance in Tla'amin did not take place until the 20th century, but the impact of settlers outside Tla'amin was felt going back to the 1860s.

1862 – Smallpox

The Covid pandemic affected all of us, but the impact on First Nations was more severe. It is not particularly surprising to First Nations people that their case rates and fatality rates were higher, nor was this a new experience for them. This disparity was the result of systemic racial and social inequality that has existed for more than 150 years. Conditions created by settler colonialism over the past 150 years have resulted in the fact that too many First Nations people continue to live in inadequate housing, lack clean water, do not have access to doctors, and lack the technology to support virtual treatment. Even when they do have access to medical services, this historical pattern of racism makes it difficult for them to trust what is being provided.

You might think we would have learned from the past, but that only works when you are taught it. The outbreak of European diseases devastated First Nations people in much of Canada in the 18th century, but First Nations on the West Coast didn't receive their first exposure until the last half of the 19th century, a time when inoculations were fully understood by settlers and widely available.

In 1862, a smallpox epidemic erupted when a ship from San Francisco, carrying 350 passengers, arrived with at least one smallpox-infected passenger. Victoria's white population had grown to 5,000 since the establishment of Fort Victoria by the Hudson's Bay Company in 1843. The First Nations population in the area at the time was of similar size, with many First Nations people travelling to and from Victoria to trade.

First Nations lived a relatively communal existence, making them particularly susceptible to smallpox.[4] The action and inaction of the white settlers, however, is what did the most damage.

The white population was inoculated and quarantined, while First Nations were intentionally left untreated. The First Nations population in Victoria went murderously uncared for. The white police forced First Nations out of their camps. They towed them up the coast in canoes filled with their infected people, and followed that by burning their Victoria camps to the ground.

At least 30,000 First Nations people died, including many in Tla'amin, from the smallpox outbreak over the next year. Tla'amin's oral history recalls that so many of their people died from the ravages of smallpox that there were not enough people alive to bury the dead. The chain of events that followed resulted in starvation and abandonment of villages, as many First Nations people saw no option other than to move to newly formed cities to work. They accepted low-paying jobs, and mistreatment, as their only option for survival. [5]

The European settlers in Victoria knew their actions would spread smallpox across British Columbia. The outbreak was just another shameful way to get rid of Indians. Their action and inaction caused widespread death and the breakdown of the socio-economic structure of First Nations people. Alcohol was introduced, diets were changed,

---

4   https://web.UVic.ca/vv/student/smallpox/overview/
        index.html; https://www.macleans.ca/news/canada/
        how-a-smallpox-epidemic-forged-modern-british-columbia/
5   https://www.ictinc.ca/blog/
        the-impact-of-smallpox-on-first-nations-on-the-west-coast

all opening the door wide for the always opportunistic Catholic Church to establish itself, and for alcoholism to spread.[6]

1868 Opportunistic Church

In 1868 Father (later Bishop) Durieu arrived in Sechelt, which today is just a ferry ride away from West Vancouver, and took advantage of the weakened state of the northern Coast Salish territory. Durieu was quoted by Edwin M. Lemert in his article "The Life and Death of an Indian State," published in 1954, saying:[7]

"The Indian is weak in heart and mind ... He must be paternally guided ... Indians are only big children ... and hence [have] need for other than regular white law and control ..."

Recognizing he did not have the numbers to have a missionary reside in each community, Durieu established a theocratic system supported by local First Nations people, including chiefs, giving them power as judges, watchmen, and police. While the priests had ultimate power, the "Indian" watchmen looked for non-compliance with the behaviours defined by Durieu. The judges judged, and the police followed through with the punishment. Durieu quickly turned members of a collaborative community against one another.

Durieu's methods were not equally effective everywhere, but they were consistently destructive. More isolated communities, including Klahoose and Homalco, were able to push back and retain some of their ways to a degree.

Under Durieu's direction, the "discretions" of taking part in traditional dance, potlatch, worship other than Catholic, and not attending church were punished. The church was cruel. They saw First Nations as inferior and expendable. They really believed this. Based on our treatment of First Nations today, maybe too many of us still do.

---

6   https://www.tlaaminnation.com/tlaamin-nation-will-fight-for-return-of-lands-after-burial-grounds-are-desecrated-by-developer-at-sɛʔaystən-emmonds-beach/

7   *Life and Death of an Indian State*, Edwin M. Lemert. Publisher: Society for Applied Anthropology. Vol 13. Nov. 3, 1954

Determining and forcing people to be something they are not, no matter how much it hurt or how much harm it caused, was what Father Durieu brought to the northern Coast Salish territory. Catholicism weakened the First Nations communities further, and then more white people showed up and took the land.

Mid 1800s – Introduction of alcohol

My wife is a recovering alcoholic, a fact I share with her permission. She is white and has been sober for most of our 30 years together, thanks in part to access to the best in rehab centres.

I learned from her experience what a short distance it can be, literally and figuratively, from a Yaletown apartment to Vancouver's downtown east side. She needed help addressing her own multigenerational trauma. A lot of pain was handed down. When she shares her story today, people have difficulty connecting the person they see with that young mom living a life that came close to putting her on the street. This experience helps me relate on some level to what Joe's life would have been like, growing up living with alcoholism.

The introduction of alcohol, timed just as First Nations communities were being devastated by disease and death, created a perfect storm that continues today.

Alcohol and abuse were prevalent in Joe's life, and addiction is still one of the main issues that challenge First Nations people while they work to reclaim their mental wellness. Joe and I had a lot of back and forth on how to address First Nations issues of alcohol and abuse. Joe chose not to share too much personal detail on the role alcohol has played in his family's life directly. Plenty of media depictions show the detrimental impact of alcohol on First Nations people as part of the colonial experience, and continue to shape stereotypes and feed racism today.

An article published in 1957 titled "The Use of Alcohol in Three Salish Indian Tribes," written by Edwin M. Lemert, Ph.D and professor of sociology at the University of California, immediately resonated with Joe. It was published not long before his birth and describes a world familiar to him: the world his parents grew up in and were living in when they started their family.

Professor Lemert wrote that, "The three tribes [Sliammon, Homalco, Klahoose] first began to be Catholicized in the 1860s, and by 1885 they had all been converted." The church forbid alcohol, and the Coast Salish had to swear off it to be converted. That didn't stop the drinking. It just moved it underground. Initially, the alcohol consumed was whisky or rum that they traded for, but eventually the people learned to make homebrew. The behaviour was primarily binge drinking as a group, rather than individual drinking. It was drinking to get drunk. This is behavior that Joe continued to witness in the community while growing up.

The article went on to discuss the behavioural changes that alcohol brought about.

"In all three tribes, drunken men in a number of instances have violently assaulted their wives, blackened their eyes and given them nasty bruises.

"Cases of seduction of young girls, resulting in illegitimate childbirth, and adulterous unions involving married women, likewise seem to have intoxication as their main concomitant. One or two cases of drunken rape are on the record.

"Within the Indian communities themselves, while there is verbal disapproval of drinking, it is inconsistent and not substantiated by social rejection or penalties of any kind. The chief has no power to punish tribe members, and the council is equally impotent to invoke penalties for misbehavior. Any effort of this nature could only stir up grudges and provoke more fractional conflict than already exists."

To be very clear, most First Nations people do not have drug and alcohol dependency issues. The reality is, however, a higher percentage of First Nations people struggle with dependency than in the general population. There is zero genetic reason for this. The higher rate of dependency can logically be tied back to multigenerational trauma. Many studies, including the work of Dr. Maria Yellow Horse Brave

Heart, clearly identify a link between the treatment of indigenous people by white settlers and the resulting "historical trauma" that has left survivors with guilt, shame, anger, and PTSD.[8] These conditions of emotional abuse, including the kind experienced in residential schools, and other neglect of children have been directly associated with drinking problems in adult survivors.[9]

Considering their experiences—the widespread loss of their land, self-determination, children and/or childhood, and overall way of life—we should be helping, not judging.

8   https://ssw.smith.edu/about/news-events/
      dr-maria-yellow-horse-brave-heart-returns-smith-give-rapoport-lecture
9   *Psychology Today*. "Childhood Trauma and Alcohol Abuse: The connection".
      Joseph Nowinski, June 2013

10. Childhood Shaped by a Lost History

Joe: *When I first started thinking about capturing and telling my history, I read and listened to several biographies and saw a common theme. They would tell a story of how their experiences shaped their later lives, starting with their family and their earliest memories. At first, when I reflected on my own family experience, I felt nothing but a void. Over the course of my life, I had been able to move ahead and tackle many challenges, but I would be always burdened by unresolved issues and trauma. To be the best I could be, I had to look backwards before I could go further forward. As I began to unpack the trauma, I gained a much better understanding of the struggles of those who came before me and how that shaped my reality growing up. They did their best, under imposed deplorable conditions, to create the opportunity for me to live a better life than they had. Now, the challenge has passed on to me to raise the bar for my son and for the future generations for them to live an even better life.*

John: As a child, Joe knew his parents were fluent speakers of the Tla'amin language. They would use it to speak to each other when they didn't want their kids to know what they were saying. They also spoke it with other adults, and Joe could only stand by, wondering what was being said. As he grew older and began working for the community in the treaty process, he learned to appreciate the value of the language and its significance to the rights and culture of the Tla'amin people. Language is a common thread that holds everything together, from identity and culture to governance and laws, to relationships with all things, including families, the land, and the rich resources within Tla'amin territory. Through language, everything in a people's world view is defined. Fluent language speakers hold traditional knowledge of their people. Joe's parents did not pass the language on to him, and he had no grandparents to teach him.

From a childhood perspective, Joe still holds anger towards his dad (Norman). There are memories marked by traumatic experiences involving him and his temper, alcohol, domestic violence, and physical and verbal abuse, all generating fear in his mother, his siblings and himself. As he continues his own journey through life, Joe accepts that he needs to work on understanding how his dad and his actions affected who he is.

Norman was shaped by his great-grandmother, Mary, who raised him along with his great-grandfather, Joe. Mary had lived through the days of early contact and saw the direct effects of the white supremacist approach. She witnessed the unjust land appropriation, the introduction of the Indian Act and the reserve system, residential schools, alcoholism, and catholicization of the community. To understand his dad, Joe was determined to also explore Mary's life experience. What was the impact of colonialism and the first white settlers? How did this shape how she raised Norman? Why was he so angry? What were their lives like? How much did the settler colonizers' treatment of First Nations people as "less than" contribute to his dad's perspectives and temper? How did these actions contribute to the loss of traditions, to family dysfunction, and rejection?

As Joe begins to answer those questions, it becomes clear that Norman's anger was unsurprising. His whole life, he was treated as "less than," yet he was always trying to prove that he was not. This included his determination to have their home on the reserve stand out due to its exceptionally clean finish, tidy yard, and nice car. He raised his children with a focus on seeing them succeed in a world that was not fair to them.

11. From Tradition to Trauma. The impact during Mary Galligos' lifetime, 1871-1962

Joe: *Mary, my great-great-grandmother, I am told by those elders that remember her, was a kind and gentle woman. I imagine that she would have been raised with the teachings and culture of the Tla'amin people at the time, which would have been very structured. My great-great-grandfather, Joe Galligos, would probably also have been familiar with that kind of structure from his time in the Chilean navy. Mary and Joe had five sons and three daughters between the years 1900 and 1912. They also raised my dad, their great-grandson, who was born in 1938. Joe and Mary would have been 67 years old when Dad was born. Joe passed away when my dad was 10, leaving Mary to raise my dad on her own at that point. I can only imagine the richness of the culture and teachings my dad was raised with, and the conflict at a time when settler colonialism was doing all it could to make all First Nations and Indigenous peoples, often referred to as "the Indian problem," disappear.*

John: A 1962 Powell River news article regarding Mary's death said, "She watched Powell River grow from the first felled tree, and the growth of the mill, its surrounding townsite and outlying districts." The main Tla'amin village was at this site. Tiys'kwat was removed, without consultation with its inhabitants, to make way for the pulp and paper mill in 1910, which still stands there today.

Besides being inaccurate in stating that Mary died at 110 years old—she would have been 90 or 91—this would not have been a happy time for the Tla'amin people, as the article implies. I can only imagine Mary's devastation at the loss of their traditional land and being restricted to the reserve, which occurred in her lifetime.

Joe's great-great-grandfather, Joe Galligos, to the left of the priest holding a baby. Reprinted with permission of qathet Museum and Archives. 1967.1.34

Joe Galligos was a member of the Chilean navy and of Spanish/ Chilean descent, who arrived in Coast Salish Territory and married into the community. He must have fit in, because he became a band member. It isn't clear why he stayed behind when his ship sailed off, but Galligos has become a proud and important name in the Tla'amin community.

Joe met Mary Adams in Steveston, at the mouth of the Fraser River, while working in a fish cannery, as many First Nations people did at that time. Mary was from the K'ómoks peoples on Vancouver Island, but due to a sickness, likely smallpox, breaking out in K'ómoks she was unable to return there. Instead, they made their way to Tla'amin. They brought the Galligos name and its various future spellings to Tla'amin. Joe and Mary were Joe kʷunəmɛn Gallagher's great-great-grandparents.

Joe Gallagher was born a Galligos, however Norman changed the family's name to Gallagher when Joe was in Grade 6. The story, as he remembers it, was about his dad's paycheques. Norman was working in a logging camp at the time. His paycheque back then was delivered by mail and often would go to the wrong Galligos mailbox. As they were a large family in Tla'amin, there were many Galligos households, and mail would often be misdelivered. He would have to go searching for it, and that was something he wasn't too happy about. Norman wasn't much fun to be around if he wasn't happy. Joe does, however, think it funny that he chose an Irish name. In doing family research, he found many old newspaper stories of Norman's great uncles playing sports, and they were often incorrectly referred to as Gallagher instead of Galligos. Perhaps that's where the alternative name came from. At more than one soccer tryout, Joe's appearance surprised people who were expecting an Irishman but got this First Nations guy instead. On the other hand, if Norman had kept the Galligos name, then people might have expected a Spanish guy!

Joe and Mary Galligos were born in 1871, just 28 years after Fort Victoria was established, and nine years following the smallpox spread. Joe died in 1948. Mary lived until 1962. She endured and was witness to many settler atrocities. She was a long-term survivor in the face of the many attempts to get rid of the "Indian problem."

Mary's lifetime spanned much of the raping of their territory and the destruction of their way of life. Imagine what her life was like. The extreme racism she would have endured while suffering through the many actions of marginalization and oppression intended to achieve cultural genocide. The Tla'amin people, like all First Nations people, were doing all they could do just to survive. Consider just how difficult it would have been to raise children at that time, and in that environment, let alone doing it while you were in your seventies.

Colonial history started earlier in Eastern Canada, but in the West, and in Tla'amin specifically, the transition from their First Nations way of life for thousands of years to the current state happened in front of Mary's eyes. She would have been witness to the full colonial experience and its impact on Tla'amin.

1871: British Columbia became a province of Canada

In the year Mary was born, despite First Nations population declines due to smallpox, they still made up most of the BC population. Regardless, they were given no role in governing or participation in the "democracy" of Canada[10]. "Indians," people who had never ceded control of their land and title rights, were placed under the control of the government.

Article 13 of the agreement making BC a province of Canada gave authority[11] over First Nations to Canada. In a departure from the agreements with other provinces, though, BC retained a veto over First Nations persons and lands. This shaped the differences in the relationships with First Nations in BC compared to the rest of Canada. The province used that veto to avoid discussing treaties, or questions of title. It also used the veto power in maintaining, and then shrinking, what were already the smallest reserves in all of Canada.[12] This is why BC lands are primarily unceded, and there are 203 "bands" in BC, accounting for almost one-third of all "bands" in Canada.

1872: Indian Agent Dr. Israel W. Powell.[13]

The town of Powell River was named after Dr. Israel W. Powell, whose duties included rounding up First Nations children and taking them to residential "schools."

I still consider Powell River my home. It was only in working on this project that I learned that the town's namesake was an Indian agent. He was also the superintendent of Indian Affairs for British Columbia for 17 years.

The *British Columbia Historical Quarterly* published in January 1947 by the British Columbia Historical Association was very

---

10   https://royalbcmuseum.bc.ca/exhibits/bc-archives-time-machine/galler07/frames/
      confed.htm
11   Challenging Racist British Columbia. 150 Years and Counting. *The Canadian
      Centre for Policy Alternatives (BC Office)*
12   https://Indigenousfoundations.arts.ubc.ca/reserves/
13   http://prvoices.org/wp-content/uploads/2014/07/Sliammon-Historical-Timeline.pdf

complimentary about Powell's achievements, stating that, "He was able to boast that in his 17 years he was able to open 17 Indian [residential] schools.[14]

"He taught the natives to obey the law, to permit the education of their children, to trust white doctors, rather than in the medicine men of tribes …"

The article went on to state that, "The work of Dr. Powell for the betterment of conditions amongst the Indians is worthy of a book."

This gives an idea of the mindset of the mainstream population back in 1947. I agree his story is worthy of being included in this book. What Dr. Powell was leading is at the heart of the impacts that so many First Nations people continue to suffer from today. He was a racist white supremacist whose injustices included the amendment to the Indian Act in 1884 to ban potlatches.

It's time for a new name for Powell River. Unfortunately, many of the current residents are resistant. I am hopeful that by the time this book is published, and as people become more educated, that will change. There is so much to be gained by accepting the past and moving forward together with respect. Changing the name does no harm to the people that live there, but it will mean a lot to the people of Tla'amin. It is a simple change and an important statement. People will adapt quickly to the new name, as we have to Haida Gwaii. There is a generation growing up today that doesn't know that Haida Gwaii was previously called something else.

1873: Lot 450 purchased illegally by close associate of Dr. Powell's

Lot 450 was composed of land stretching from xak"um (Grief Point, where I grew up) to Tla'amin. This land today makes up most of the municipality of Powell River and comprises 14 kilometres of beautiful coastline. It held villages and numerous seasonal camping areas for Tla'amin people at the time it was taken.

---

14   http://www.library.ubc.ca/archives/pdfs/bchf/bchq_1947_1.pdf

White settlers were given free land in traditional Tla'amin territory and became rich off the land and its resources. First Nations were nonparticipants.

1875: 320 acres made available for free to white settlers

There was more available for purchase. There was no option made available to First Nations. The land was taken away from underneath the Tla'amin people and given to someone else to build on.

Rupert Ross, author of *Indigenous Healing*[15], tells a story that was passed on to him from an Elder. A short version of that story goes something like this. *"We used to hold up our hands high and pray with our eyes open. The white man told us we should hold our hands down, bow our head and close our eyes to pray. So, we gave it a try. When we opened our eyes again, our land was gone."*

1876: First version of the Indian Act passed

The Indian Act is racist and oppressive federal legislation that exists to this day. It was introduced to facilitate the assimilation of "Indians" as part of the colonial approach to resolve the "Indian problem." It was designed to eliminate First Nations.

The people in Tla'amin became wards of the Canadian government. Being a ward is normally associated with children, and in many ways that is how they were treated. They were told that the land that they had lived on for thousands of years was now owned by someone else. Perhaps it is more accurate to describe them as *prisoners*, since for many years, they needed permission just to leave the reserve. With little access to land, they were forced to live off the sea, whose resources were being devastated by white settler development. The Tla'amin people's treatment

---

15   *Indigenous Healing. Exploring Traditional Paths.* Rupert Ross. Published by Penguin Group

was the colonist's best guess at what was just good enough to lead to their goal of genocide through assimilation.

The colonizers limited travel between villages, which would have separated Mary from her family in K'ómoks as well as from her people in Klahoose, Homalko and likely Sechelt and other parts of the Coast Salish Nation. The ocean was their transportation system, and it had kept these villages connected until the settlers arrived.

The Act divided First Nations communities already weakened by disease into small bands. Imagine a small community of people that were unable to leave the reserve and the impact this restriction would have on their ability to maintain a population level.

Restricting the Tla'amin people to reserves supported the government aims of keeping them away from their old territories. Settlers were able to capitalize on their resources without them getting in the way. The reserve system used in Canada gained such a reputation among colonizers that it became the model South Africa used in developing their infamous apartheid system.

The Indian Act was particularly cruel to First Nations women. It ignored First Nations hereditary ways, where women shared equal responsibilities, and imposed a colonial patriarchal society, profoundly enabling the marginalization of First Nations women. This ensured that First Nations women were discriminated against not only for being Indigenous, but also for being women. When an "Indian" man married a non-Indian, he and his wife would have "status" under the Act, but if an Indian woman married a non-Indian, she would lose her status. The passing of status to children was granted based only on paternal status. Among many other issues, this made it very difficult for battered women to leave their homes, as Joe grew up experiencing. The loss of status for women marrying non-status men continued until 1985.

1885: Indian Act outlawed potlatches and other First Nations ceremonies, with non-compliance punishable by jail time.[16]

The Potlatch Law, through an amendment to the Indian Act led by Israel Powell, made potlatches and other cultural gatherings illegal. It remained in place until 1951.

This prohibition on gatherings prevented First Nations from legally passing down their oral history and their teachings, their ways of handling disputes and of being respectful. Historic gatherings were banned, with the intent that Christianity would fill the void.

Historic practices have started to return, and younger First Nations people are gaining this critical knowledge and understanding. Knowing their language and teachings has given people far more strength and self-esteem than Joe grew up with.

If you are interested in learning more about the Indian Act, there are many great books that have been written on the subject, including *21 Things You May Not Know About the Indian Act*, by Bob Joseph.

1891: British Columbia white population outnumbers First Nations for the first time

When the white population began to overtake the First Nations, it was more the result of a declining First Nations population than an increase in settlers.

The pre-contact population of BC First Nations has been estimated at between 80,000 and 125,000 people.

The total British Columbia population in 1891 was approximately 98,000,[17] with the majority being white. The white population was growing, while the loss of First Nations people in those years was absolutely devastating, including in Tla'amin.

---

16   *21 Things You May Not Know About the Indian Act*. Bob Joseph
17   https://www.bac-lac.gc.ca/eng/census/1891/Pages/about-census.aspx

By 1929, following years of disease and colonial action to get rid of the "Indian problem," the First Nations population in BC had declined to 22,000[18].

1896: Catholic Church built in Tla'amin

Even today, the church remains prominent in Tla'amin. With the establishment of the church, all First Nations regalia was hidden or destroyed. The knowledge and traditions that were retained were hidden from the church and kept underground.

This created a shift in how the Tla'amin people valued themselves. They were being forced away from traditional values. Their spiritual beliefs were under attack. There was a new set of rules to live by, or else they were deemed to be sinners. The main reason to be labelled a sinner was to be "Indian" in how they raised their kids, how they lived their lives, and even how they thought. The church arrived in the centre of the community at a time when the Tla'amin people had already been corralled by the government. They were simply desperate to survive.

Joe was raised Catholic, attending the church that was built to be the focal point of their community. He was fully involved through his childhood: he was baptized, served as an altar boy, and went to confession, confirmation, and catechism. He was raised as a Catholic Indian child.

Joe's mom, Ann, went to church, but Norman didn't. He fell out with the church because he didn't believe in what they were saying and wouldn't conform. This didn't stop him from seeking help from a priest, though. There were times when Norman would abuse Ann, and then she would pack her three kids up and take them on the bus down to Vancouver. She wanted to escape that abusive life with Norman. Eventually, Norman would come down to Vancouver with the support of the local priest, who would explain to Ann that she needed to keep the family together. The priest told Ann that was God's will. They

---

18   https://www.fnha.ca/wellness/our-history-our-health

needed to work it out. It was these values and actions that made Joe begin to hate the church.

As much as Ann was trying to hold her family together, Joe knew they were never going to be a happy one. It was never going to be anything but dysfunctional. Why did they keep going back and forth? Most of Ann's siblings lived in Vancouver, so it made some sense why she went there. Joe understood life in the city was tough, but it was about picking the lesser of two evils. He didn't want to see his mom get hurt repeatedly.

When Norman got his family back to Tla'amin, he'd be better for a while. He did want his family to be together, but he lacked a "normal" family upbringing to base it on. The priest would go over and try to counsel Norman and Ann to try to maintain some peace, but eventually the behaviour would return, and back to Vancouver they would go.

The priest, along with a few members of the RCMP, was the only white man Joe remembers coming to their house in the 1960s. The priest was a presence in the community, just as the Indian agents must have been for the Tla'amin community when the reserve was first established.

For all the time Ann lived in Tla'amin, she continued to go to church. She didn't know anything else, having started during her years in a Catholic residential school.

The last time Joe attended church was for midnight mass, his first Christmas home from university. The church was full. The priest started lecturing everyone for not attending more regularly. Joe was already angry at the Church and challenging its values. That was the last service Joe chose to go to. He hated it for so many reasons, and yet at that point he still didn't fully comprehend the impact the Church had had on the lives of First Nations people.

1910 to 1915: First Nations forcibly removed from Lot 450; mill construction starts

The Tla'amin people's first direct contact with Europeans is believed to have come in 1792, when Captain George Vancouver sailed his two ships past Ahgykson Island (Vancouver renamed it Harwood Island at the time, but as a provision of the Sliammon treaty it was renamed Ahgykson in 2016). Significant white settlement didn't occur on traditional Tla'amin territory, however, until the early 20th century, when construction of the paper mill and dam started.

In the first few pages of a book I have on Powell River's history, *Pulp, Paper and People. 75 Years of Powell River*,[19] Page 5 celebrates "Powell River's first white settler." Page 7 has a photo of the "first known white girl born in Powell River." I was surprised by the direct reference to the "white" people. When I first read the book in 1988, I didn't even notice First Nations were excluded.

Scanning the index, I found multiple references to Sliammon. The first one, on page 2, stated,

"At spawning time in the fall, the Sliammon Indians rowed their dugouts from their village north of Wildwood and camped at the mouth of Powell River as they had for at least 2,000 years, fishing and drying the rich catch of salmon. The fish were so plentiful then it was possible to cross the river on their backs, but in less than a decade they were completely gone." That's it. No mention that the mill was built on their village site. No mention of the dam that turned Powell River into Powell Lake and flooded traditional territory; no mention that the settlers were the reason the salmon disappeared. In fact, without starting a new paragraph, the next sentence talks about all the new money coming into Powell River.

Oh well, the fish were gone. At least we have money.

Pulp, Paper and People is a book about white people. It isn't that First Nations are treated as "less than" in this book on Powell River's

---

19   *Pulp Paper and People. 75 Years of Powell River*, Karen Southern, Peggy Bird. Published 1988

history. Rather, they are almost invisible. In reading further, I learned that I delivered the newspaper to the man that owned a pub near the mill which barred First Nations people even after the law said they were allowed in pubs. We were ignorant. It's clear that growing up in this environment influenced how many of us think today, even if it is unconscious bias. I keep learning of the many blind spots I still have.

The damming of Powell River created Powell Lake, which is 51 kilometres long, with 480 kilometres of shoreline. It is one of the deepest lakes in British Columbia and is lined with beautiful cabins owned by white people.

Along with damming the river and destroying much of their hunting area, the government also allocated forest use for logging through a tenure system to "white" companies. Many First Nations people held jobs in the logging industry, and in the fishery, but it was others that made the real money off their unceded territory. I have personally benefited from working for three of the largest forest companies in BC.

The Powell River Pulp and Paper Mill became the largest producer of newsprint in the world in the 1960s and 1970s. Powell River became a wonderful, rich town for white people to grow up in. I am one of them. The people of Tla'amin were not invited to participate, despite the fact that the resources that drove the riches came from their traditional territory.

It only took a short time for the Tla'amin people's way of life to be decimated, in a pattern that has been repeated across First Nations communities in Canada. It wasn't just a loss of trees. They lost an entire ecosystem. Habitats were destroyed, killing fish, wildlife, plant life, and berries.

Hunting and fishing for Tla'amin people wasn't just a matter of taking from the land and the sea. They were stewards, preserving what was needed for future generations. Fishing, from a First Nations perspective, is not just throwing a rod in the water and hoping to catch a fish. It is about taking care of the environment and the habitat and respecting the spirit of the animal being taken. They were taught not to waste. Even how they prepared to hunt or fish was important. They didn't just buy a gun and start shooting. I can only imagine how it would have pained Mary and others when the salmon disappeared from the mouth of Powell River within 10 years of the mill construction starting. The herring that used to be plentiful for generations in front of the Tla'amin community also disappeared.

1920 – Infamous quote from Duncan Campbell Scott, deputy superintendent of Indian Affairs[20]

While making residential schools mandatory for Indian children in Canada ages five to 17, Duncan Campbell Scott said: "I want to get rid of the Indian problem … Our objective is to continue until there is not an Indian that has not been absorbed into the body politic, and there is no Indian question, and no Indian Department. That is the whole object of this bill."

Residential schools were one of the main implements of the colonial governments to get rid of the "Indian problem." The harm they caused is finally getting attention from Canadians. These institutions were not schools. They were designed to break down the First Nations family structure by mandating that children be taken from their parents, to then "kill the Indian in the child."

Norman spent just one year in residential school, and after that, somehow he stayed away from it. The remainder of his schooling was in Indian day schools, which had their own set of issues. Ann was in residential school from a young age until she was 15. All this shaped Joe's life growing up on Sliammon Indian Band Reserve #1. By the time he was born, attendance at residential school was no longer mandatory, so his parents sent him to public school in Powell River. However, the intergenerational traumas from residential school and other colonial experiences were real for his parents as survivors, and for Joe and his siblings as children of survivors. You can't help but become a product of your environment—good and bad. The Indian

---

20   *21 Things You Didn't know about the Indian Act*. Bob Joseph

Act is still in place today; racism and oppression are alive and well. First Nations are still working to survive.

Joe saw and lives with the direct impact residential schools had on his parents' lives and that of so many around them. On reflection, it shouldn't surprise anyone that Norman pushed his family to focus on assimilation. He was coerced into having his children focus on becoming part of the white world.

Finally, by the time the Truth and Reconciliation Commission settlement was determined, and people started talking about the atrocities of residential schools and other First Nations abuses, Norman and Ann were already gone. They had grown up without a mom and dad, leaving Joe and his siblings without grandparents. They had lived their entire lives in a period of denial.

1927: Indian Act amendment prevents First Nations from hiring, or having someone hire, legal representatives

The Indian Act was amended to make it illegal for Indians to hire a lawyer or to give someone money to hire a lawyer. Nothing says "you have a case" more clearly than making it illegal for the law to be contested. It took tremendous time and effort to catch up, in terms of formalizing the BC First Nations legal case.

1929: First Chief and Council system enforced in Tla'amin

The chief and council system replaced the existing hereditary system of governance. This happened in the late 1800s in most of Canada, with the passing of the Indian Act.

Prior to the enforcement of the Act, every nation had their own historic governance structure. Hereditary leaders were responsible for rights and title. People learned by listening to and watching the knowledge carriers, and then by practicing and doing. Learning started at a young age and was a multigenerational, lifelong process. Everyone had their roles in the community, and they contributed through an efficient and effective First Nations society.

These existing First Nations governance systems were defined by First Nations peoples to govern their interests throughout their entire territories and over all affairs of their peoples and relations with other First Nations. Their existence was managed through recognition that First Nations laws and spirituality are as one with the land.

This hereditary governance system was replaced by an elected chief and council system with a two-year term, which was a system familiar to colonists and was imposed as a way to further the attack on First Nations societies.

Little attempt was made by colonists to understand First Nations' systems of governance that had long pre-existed contact. First Nations people were simply perceived as inferior and in the way of settlers' interests.

Unlike the hereditary system, where leaders were trained their entire lives to take on their roles, the imposed systems have often turned neighbour against neighbour, family against family, and even split families. It isn't uncommon to have five individuals running for chief. The candidate with the most votes wins, so it is quite likely that a minority will determine the winner. In a small community, elected leaders who don't have the support of a majority have a big challenge ahead of them, especially with many terms being only two years. Despite good intentions, it is difficult for community leaders to create effective and sustainable change with their limited power, scope, and short terms.

As with the governance actions of Father Durieu in the 19th century, the chief and council system often leads to deep divisions in First Nations societies that historically operated through consensus-building. The system lacks proper representation, has limited resources, and lacks continuity. It is dysfunctional and causes harm.

The chief and council are elected by the community, but they operate on behalf of the federal government, as many have said, to "administer their own poverty." They put First Nations people into positions where they need to provide bureaucratic answers to their own people for unmet needs.

Having a system that elects a chief and council every two years is not only divisive but results in people having to do politicking almost constantly, which is not conducive to the stability required to create and achieve a long-term vision for the people.

1948: UN Convention on the Prevention and Punishment of the Crime of Genocide signed by 152 countries, including Canada

Canada has been in denial about its treatment of First Nations. Genocide, as defined in the UN Convention, means "any of the following acts committed with intent to destroy, in whole or in part, a national, ethnical, racial, or religious group:

- Killing members of the group;
- Causing serious bodily or mental harm to members of the group;
- Deliberately inflicting on the group conditions of life calculated to bring about its physical destruction in whole or in part;
- Imposing measures intended to prevent births within the group;
- Forcibly transferring children of the group to another group."

The mention of genocide leads me to think of Germany, the Balkans, and Rwanda, but in Canada's case it happened in my own community. I hadn't even considered Canada in the discussion. Yet, the government of Canada openly campaigned and put genocidal legislation in place to get rid of the "Indian problem."

Germany, by law, does not allow denial of their genocide, and it is an important part of their school curriculum. In Canadian schools, we haven't until recently acknowledged our historic treatment of

First Nations. The truth must become a more significant element of our education system.

As Canadians, we promote ourselves as leaders in human rights. We are quick to point out the faults of other countries, but we have failed at looking inward. Consider the United Nations Declaration on Indigenous Peoples (UNDRIP) that was approved by the UN in 2007 with only four dissenting votes. Canada was one of those four. Following the release of the Truth and Reconciliation Report in 2015, Canada finally signed on to UNDRIP. Even that hasn't stopped the federal government from fighting against interpretations of it actively in federal courts.

Pushing off dealing with our treatment of First Nations is hardly new. In a report by the UN Human Rights committee on Canada in 1999[21], Canada was heavily criticized for not following through on its commitments made in the 1996 Royal Commission on Aboriginal Peoples (RCAP). As a country, we seem all too happy to just keep kicking this can down the road without taking the "decisive and urgent action" needed in support of the RCAP recommendations the UN called for. We need truth and action.

1949: First Nations individuals given the right to vote in provincial elections.

1951: First Nations people gain legal access to beer parlours for the first time, although not all businesses complied.

In 1970, the Supreme Court upheld the rights of First Nations members to drink in public establishments. In Powell River, Tla'amin women were allowed in designated areas in pubs only until 3 p.m.

---

21   *Concluding observations of the Human Rights Committee: Canada. 07/04/99*

1951 – Indian Act amended to remove restriction on First Nations legal representation

The 1951 amendment to the Indian Act gave First Nations the ability to have legal representation and, therefore, the ability to start challenging their treatment. Because of the unique situation in British Columbia, which was primarily unceded territory, many BC cases were brought to the Supreme Court. It has been a long, difficult process.

First Nations faced many roadblocks in creating their own representation to challenge colonial laws. It wasn't until 1961 that a First Nations person was called to the bar in BC. Hereditary Chief of the Kwikwasutinuxw Alfred Scow[22] graduated from the University of British Columbia law school and went on to serve as a judge in the BC Provincial Court.

1960: First Nations given right to vote in federal elections

1961: Joe Gallagher and John Matterson born

1962: Mary Galligos dies at 92

Mary was witness to massive infringements of her First Nations rights. Far too many First Nations lives were needlessly lost in her lifetime. These actions, and inactions, continue to have a significant negative impact on her descendants, including Joe, her great-great-grandson.

---

22   https://historyproject.allard.ubc.ca/law-history-project/profile/honourable-alfred-j-scow-oc-obc

Part 3

JOE'S PARENTS

12. You Can't Get Ahead Living Like an Indian

Joe: *Status Indians and Indian reserves are a creation of the Indian Act. It not only established Status Indians as wards of the federal government but confined us to the Indian reserve to intensify control over all aspects of our lives, as a major instrument of genocide to finally solve the Indian problem. The options were basically to assimilate or stay on the reserve and die.*

Life on the Tla'amin Reserve defined my childhood and shaped how I grew up. There was the ugly side that exposed itself too often, a side that instilled fear and shame that I couldn't hide from or avoid getting stuck in. There was an environment in the community shaped by settler colonialism that was working to ensure First Nations people from different communities would end up in the same way. I didn't know that I wasn't learning about my identity. Instead, I was learning about a path towards assimilation to survive.

John: Joe knew so little about Tla'amin culture and teachings that he didn't know he was Coast Salish until he was 10. He was attending James Thompson Elementary School in Powell River, and all the students were organized into house teams that would compete against each other within the school. The teams were named after three different "Indian" nations from eastern Canada, the Cree, Mohawk, and Iroquois. He was Iroquois. That was the only "Indian" identity he knew at the time. He didn't know what nation the Sliammon Band was part of. Eventually, he started playing on a soccer team based on the reserve and coached by Joe Mitchell that was called Coast Salish. He asked what that was, and Mitchell told Joe that's what he was. He learned a lot from Joe Mitchell.

My elementary school, at the other end of Powell River, had similar team names, but ours were at least West Coast–based. I remember our teams being Haida, Nootka and Salish. Ironically, I was Salish. I didn't know that Salish was what the people in Sliammon were, either.

I knew Joe Mitchell from playing soccer with his son Gary on a Powell River team, before I played with Joe. Joe Mitchell was one of the nicest men Joe had ever met, and while I didn't spend that much time around him, I had the same impression. He was gentle, and he liked to laugh and share stories about life and Coast Salish teachings. He was exemplifying what he learned and was sharing. He was an influence in Joe's life as his first soccer coach, as chief of the Sliammon Indian Band, as the band administrator, and as a Traditional Advisor for the Sliammon treaty process.

Gradually Joe learned a few more things, such as the fact his mother, Ann, was from Homalco, which is north of Tla'amin. There were others who were from elsewhere—like Joe Mitchell, whose family was from Klahoose—but were members of the Sliammon Indian Band. It just depended on which band list the government put them on. The government officials of the day did not care how the various First Nations people were connected to one another at the time when they were establishing Indian bands and setting out Indian reserve lands for those bands. If they had recognized these communities as part of the same nation, they would have seen Tla'amin, Homalko, Klahoose, and Comox together as parts of a single nation, with a common language. Of course, the government's approach to Indian bands ranged from promoting assimilation to outright genocide where eliminating culture wasn't enough. Dividing people and disrupting the existing nation-state would have fit their objectives.

Hunting, fishing, and gathering to access traditional foods and medicines in a resource-rich Tla'amin territory was essential and had sustained the Tla'amin people for thousands of years. When Joe was growing up, there were many fishermen in the community who would fish with gill nets, and some who still owned fishing vessels and participated in the fisheries every fishing season. He saw these practices and opportunities diminish substantially within his childhood years.

Norman had a little speedboat, and he liked to be out on the water with his friend Les Adams, along with his wife and family. Their son Evan is now Dr. Evan Adams, whom Joe had the opportunity to work with when he became the deputy provincial health officer for the Province of British Columbia and then the chief medical officer for the First Nations health Authority. Their families would spend time together when they were young, which created some of Joe's fondest childhood memories. They would head out in the boat for picnics to Ahgykson Island, a short trip from Tla'amin and one of their reserve land parcels. They would play all day there on the beaches.

Norman enjoyed sport fishing. He liked to be out on the water fishing and would often enter fishing derbies. As kids, Joe and his siblings would take turns going with him as his helper. Joe learned to love being out on the water and seeing the beautiful territory from the ocean. This usually meant being up early, and Norman could be a bit cranky at times, especially as his children were learning to net the fish on the line. But they liked learning things about the boat and fishing.

Norman did teach Joe and his brother about catching dog salmon that went up the river next to where they lived, using a gaff hook at the end of a long pole. Every fall, the river would rise and be full of dog salmon returning to spawn. Joe found this amazing to see, and it provided an opportunity to learn about how important this fishery was to the community. Eventually there was a salmon hatchery established in the river to enhance fish stocks in the territory.

Regrettably, Joe never had a chance to experience hunting with his dad. He wanted to learn how to handle a rifle and shoot, catch, and clean a deer. It was a big part of what a lot of other boys his age were doing. Even back then, he felt he was missing out on something that he would learn later is an important part of Tla'amin culture and rich in teachings.

Norman was a hunter. He would go hunting with his friends, but he also had a rifle with him when they went out in the boat fishing. He would shoot from the boat if he saw a deer, and then go onshore to get it. Joe also recalls staying on the boat overnight while Norman went hunting on one of the islands. That's the closest he got to hunting. They often had deer meat in the house, but the kids didn't eat much of it. When they did, it was mostly served in a stew. Norman and Ann ate a lot of seafood: salmon, prawns, and shellfish. But mostly it was just the adults. The kids usually had bologna and wieners and stuff like that. A long way from the Tla'amin traditional diet.

When they were a little older, and seafood was served, it was difficult. They hadn't acquired a taste for it. Over the years, Joe learned to enjoy salmon, cod, prawns, crab, and other such foods, however he still struggles a bit with clams and hasn't developed a palate for fish-head soup or oysters, especially if they are raw.

Coast Salish people traditionally had eaten food from the sea and all things from the land, so it seemed that Norman had a motive not to encourage his kids to eat it. Norman was adamant, "You have to learn how to live in the white world if you want to get ahead." This went along with no teaching of history, language, or culture. Norman was clear on how he was raising his family, at a time when he had to do his best to navigate the ongoing and persistent influences and impacts of colonization.

Norman was involved in the leadership of the community as an elected councillor in the 1960s, and then again when he got older. He would have been very aware of the emerging political situation of the day and the potential impacts colonial actions would have on his family and community.

1969 – Prime Minister Pierre Trudeau and Indian Affairs Minister Jean Chretien propose repeal of the Indian Act

The 1969 White Paper,[23] formally called the Statement of the Government of Canada on Indian Policy, was intended to eliminate all references to Aboriginal people in Canadian law and erase the special relationship between Canada and Indigenous peoples. It was

---

23   https://Indigenousfoundations.arts.ubc.ca/the_white_paper_1969/

yet another message from the federal government to First Nations to give up their identity. Despite the White Paper being dropped due to Aboriginal resistance, one can see where Norman might have wanted to focus on getting his children ready to compete in a white world.

Joe: *I remember the sharp voice of my father forcefully telling me that it didn't matter that I was brown; I had to learn how to be white, and in fact be twice as good as whites if I was ever to be accepted. This reflected his own painful experience with settler colonialism. He was confirming that we were being treated as "less than." Not that we* were *"less than," although that was hard to differentiate as a child or a teenager.*

John: The White Paper ended up becoming very much a focal point that brought First Nations groups together across the country. The measures were yet another clear attempt to get rid of the "Indian problem" and to tear down pre-existing First Nations government, society, and family structures.

On reflection, Joe now sees part of that legacy in how these measures convinced his father to do the government's bidding for them. He loved his children and did what he felt was best to protect them from what he had experienced. He truly wanted them to live a better life than he had. Although he was raised with a wealth of traditional knowledge and teachings, his lived experience in this settler colonial environment told him not to grow the Indian in the child. Instead, he pushed his kids to live in the white world that was taking over. He determined that they would go to school with the white kids, which fortunately meant that they would not go to residential school, but rather be integrated into public school. He also was very serious about boys learning to play sports and girls to play music. They did not learn about Tla'amin teachings, to speak the Tla'amin language, or spend time out on the land learning traditional activities like hunting. As a family, they were often isolated in their own community and even within their own extended family.

As part of the journey we are on, Joe has been able to get past some of his anger and come to recognize that his dad was doing the best he could with what he knew. With all that he had experienced and was observing, he didn't see value for his children learning the ways of the Tla'amin people. If they were going to survive in the world as it was, they would have to find success in the white world. He was clear that they were never going to climb over white people in society, but that they would have to be at their best to just survive. White people had an unfair advantage from the get-go and continued to drive it in with their discriminatory policies.

In his youth, Joe didn't experience a community-based approach to teaching an understanding of their language and culture. There was no traditional building for ceremonies, such as a long house, or classes for language. He wasn't aware of any visible ceremonial practices, like giving of Tla'amin names, rites-of-passage ceremonies, or memorials, etc. Kids his age were dependent on their parents and grandparents to teach them.

There was one significant exception to Norman not wanting to pass on Tla'amin teachings to Joe. For some reason, when Joe turned 13, Norman became adamant that he needed to learn to bathe in the river. Joe didn't understand at the time that this was a rite of passage at that age, to have a spirit bath and cleanse himself and strengthen his mind, body, and spirit. Joe had no idea what Norman was talking about, so it ended up in a big fight. Besides feeling like his dad was picking some random ceremony, Joe saw two huge issues with it. For one, Joe was born in November. It was cold outside. And, as if that wasn't enough to put him off, fish run up the river in fall, so in November there are dead carcasses decaying all around. It was too cold and too smelly. There was no way he was going to do it. It ended as another huge battle with his dad. Joe refused to do it. At least, not yet.

Being disconnected from their culture, language, and teachings made it difficult to feel proud to be First Nations in the colonial society.

13. A Hard Man, A Hard Life

Joe: *When I think about what I got from Dad, the most positive thing I can think of is his work ethic. He always worked hard, which was probably instilled by his great-grandmother. He also had strong opinions and was very stubborn. I think I have had to have some of that, too, to overcome the many challenges I have encountered in the white world. I wish there was more I could have learned from him, from what he would have acquired from her and other Knowledge Keepers who would have shared with him. However, I have also spent most of my life affirming my commitment to not be like him in so many other ways.*

John: Norman was always a hard worker, and despite the trauma he must have struggled with, he always showed up to work. He spent many years in the logging industry and ran his own business at one point. He always tried to do his best to provide. He always had a nice home, a good car, and a good boat.

While Norman had some positive attributes, to Joe they were overshadowed by his temper and how he treated his wife and his kids. He seemed annoyed or on the verge of being mad all the time. Other members of the family were walking on eggshells every day. Joe was determined he wasn't going to be angry, although as a boy he learned to get mad so he wouldn't be scared, sad or just numb! The toughest part for him was watching how his father treated Joe's mom. He was abusive. Joe was trying to figure out how to defend her. He was the oldest boy, right? His dad had instilled ideas in his head of who he *didn't* want to be.

This history of Joe's family is similar to the histories others have related many times, about life on the reserve and the impact of residential schools, alcohol, lateral violence, and colonialism. Joe is hesitant to speak specifically to a lot of these issues because it is still triggering for him and his family. He is still working on unpacking a lot of these difficult memories.

Abuse was a common thing in households. Why those men did what they did is difficult to accept, but it is clearly the result of the breakdown of families and people affected by ongoing settler colonialism.

Joe: *There really wasn't a positive Tla'amin identity, outside of sports, I can recall from my childhood. There was the stereotypical violence and bullying, and I was on the receiving end.*

14. Resilience and Achievement

Joe: *My mom, Ann, was a very kind, gentle woman. She was also very determined and resilient. At 35 years old, in 1979 she received her GED (high school equivalency) the same year I graduated from high school. In her sixties she graduated from the University of British Columbia with a degree in Social Work. Mom was full of heart and found a way through against the greatest of odds.*

John: Ann, along with all her siblings, were and are survivors of residential school. She demonstrated her will to be a survivor throughout her entire life.

Ann was in residential school at a young age. She lost her mom early in her life, and living at home with her dad was not a safe option. Being part of a broken family, residential school became the only option. At the age of six, Ann went to the Sechelt Residential School with some of her siblings, while others went to the Mission Residential School. Ann was in Sechelt until she was 14 years old.

Joe's grandfather, Ann's dad, passed away in the spring just before she met Norman. She had just turned 15, and he would have been 21 at the time and probably working in the logging industry. She married Norman shortly after they met and was still 15 when she had Joe's sister, 17 when Joe was born, and 19 when his brother arrived. It's hard to imagine what that transition was like for her.

Ann and Norman

One can only assume it was better than being at residential school. Joe's parents never talked about those days or anything personal about their past. They seemed to only want to talk about what was happening today.

Her marriage to Norman had its many challenges and caused her great harm, but raising her children provided her with a sense of purpose. She was committed to providing a home and raising her children through to the completion of Grade 12, no matter what she had to endure. She was providing them with something special that she never had. As her children were gaining on the milestone of high school graduation, the question of what life would be like with just her and Norman became a new reality. She began a difficult time in her life's journey when Joe left for university. While he was relieved to be out of the house and at university in Victoria, Joe still worried about his mom, for good reason. Just after the Christmas break, when he was back at school, he received a call from home in the late evening. He immediately organized himself to leave Victoria in the middle of the night, early enough to make the four-hour drive to Comox to catch the 7 a.m. ferry to Powell River to pick up his mom and take her to Vancouver. Norman had physically abused Ann again. Joe got in and out of Tla'amin without seeing his dad. He was still trying to protect her, and he felt angry and helpless every time this happened. Once again, though, because Joe's younger brother was still at home, she would return to the house. Her job wasn't done yet.

Later that year, Joe's brother moved to Victoria to live with Joe and attend high school to complete Grade 12. Ann had always said she would go back no matter how bad Norman was, to keep the family together and see it through until everyone had graduated. With Joe's brother living with him, some of that responsibility was passed on to Joe, and now all three of her kids were away.

She was living on a ledge emotionally and needed to decide what she wanted to do with her life. She moved to East Vancouver, and this time she wasn't going back.

Norman followed her to Vancouver, and they stayed together for a quite a while, but their relationship was as fragile as ever. Ann was able to find work with the Vancouver Police Department working as a Native liaison; this was probably a result of the initial training and work she did for the Sliammon Indian Band in the social development department. This lasted for a few years; however, the emotional toll was catching up with her. Joe's parents drank a lot when they were kids but had always been able to pull it together for the most part when they had to function. At this point, alcohol got the better of Ann. It was even to the point where Norman didn't want to be around her, and I imagine she let him know how she felt about how he had treated her all those years. It was a scary time as the alcohol consumed her life and her sense of purpose was gone.

Joe went to visit her, and she shared with him her feeling that her role as a mother was no longer required. That was a terrifying conversation for Joe. He tried to convey how important she was to her kids, even as adults, but she couldn't see her role beyond what it had been. Her own childhood without parents or grandparents contributed to her difficulty in envisioning a future role in her family's lives, as well as all the trauma and harm she had endured up to that point. Their family had been broken through colonial impacts, and this left her empty and hurt and turning to alcohol to cope.

Ann and Norman separated for good in the mid-1990s. It was a difficult time for their family. Joe's son, Benjamin, was born in 1996, and Ann was still drinking heavily. Joe remembers this because he was worried about having her around him. Joe was clear that he wasn't going to expose his child to alcohol, the way he had experienced as a child. Yet he so much wanted his son to know his grandmother and have her to play that important role in his life which Joe didn't have growing up. He did what he could to help his mom, but he couldn't allow her to be near him when she was drinking, which broke his heart.

Joe talked to his sister a lot, and they would look for ways to help their mom. Then, one day, Ann just decided to leave East Vancouver and went to live in Ottawa with Joe's sister and her family. She had made up her mind that she was going to get sober. While she was there, she simply quit—and never drank again. She had found incredible strength and the will to get on with her healing journey.

Ann came back to Vancouver after a year or two and went back to school. She completed a program at the Native Education Centre, then went on to Langara College, and eventually got her Bachelor of Social Work degree from UBC when she was in her early sixties. She was living her best life, after everything she had endured.

Ann graduating from UBC, with Joe proudly at her side.

She lived with her sister Florence. Joe's sister and Joe helped by doing what they could to make sure they had a nice place to live. Grandma was back, and it was amazing to have her there for her children and her eight grandchildren!

Joe was happy that he was now being asked to help his mom deal with simple, "normal" things, such as problems with the software on her laptop.

After she graduated, Ann started working in an organization in New Westminster, helping families and counseling battered women. She did very well in the end. All those around her were proud of her, and she was proud, too. She did everything the way she wanted, and no one could tell her otherwise.

Despite her successes, Ann still had her demons. When Norman died in 2005, they had been apart for close to 10 years. At that point, Joe's brother and his family were living with their dad in his house in Tla'amin. Ann had intended never to return to that house again—it carried too many memories and triggered too much trauma. When Norman passed, Ann came for the funeral. She was shaking but also determined to enter the house again—and she did it. She was finally able to let go. She could now freely travel to visit Joe's brother and her grandchildren, living in the house where she had endured so much.

Both of Joe's parents passed at a relatively young age because of their hard experiences. Ann and Norman came to the end of their lives apart, but through all their challenges they both came to reflect their best selves. They were survivors, doing the best they could with what they were given, and left their children in a better place than they had experienced for themselves.

Ann in particular was an inspiration; she would do anything for her children regardless of the cost to herself. She and Joe's sister had both faced unfair disadvantages as First Nations women.

The violence that First Nations women experience is often at the hands of First Nations men. This was not the case before colonization. This type of violence is known as "lateral violence." It is the manifestation of the shame and anger felt by an oppressed people and the loss of their value system.

The shame and anger clearly traces back to the introduction of alcohol, needing permission to leave a reserve, shame perpetuated by the church, and the church's insistence on keeping dysfunctional families together.

The Indian Act and its sexist rules made it difficult for women to leave their abusive husbands. First Nations women could not go to the police, the church, or the health system, as they weren't to be trusted. They couldn't go to social services, for fear their children would be taken away. Far too many First Nations women are still stuck facing violence when, only a few generations before them, women were seen as equal members of their communities.

First Nations are re-establishing some of their history in this regard and recognizing that women were, and are, highly accomplished and powerful decision-makers. This doesn't mean they are all healthy yet. There is still a long way to go and a lot of work to be done.

Joe was fortunate to grow up with such a strong mother, who endured what she did and still achieved all she did in school, her career, and her sobriety.

Part 4

SOCCER – MORE THAN JUST A GAME

15. Finding a Soccer Identity

Joe: *Soccer provided a means for me to develop a Tla'amin identity and to learn traditional teachings. Teachings I came to understand through soccer and have been able to apply to my life outside of soccer:*
- *Honour those who came before you*
- *Work ethic*
- *Manage your fear*
- *Be your best*
- *Trust in the team*
- *Humility*
- *Leave the team in a better place*

John: Tla'amin culture wasn't readily shared in Joe's family. Other people in the community had it passed on to them, to varying degrees. The parts of their culture that were retained are what has pulled them through the past 150 years and allowed them to survive. A lot of their culture has been forgotten.

Soccer played a huge role in bringing some of Tla'amin culture, language, and pride back, initially for the men and more recently for women. They were able to rediscover some of their identity as warriors, and as brave and strong people. Soccer gave them a way to apply their teachings, providing many lessons that helped them prepare for life. If you digitally search Tla'amin history in the media back to the start of the 20th century, soccer comes up as the most common result. On one hand, this is a testament to the excellence of their athletes; on the other, it shows that they were otherwise invisible.

Tla'amin Sports Heroes – Honour those who came before you

Joe: *With so much of who we were having been taken away from us and being constantly thought of and treated as the bottom of society, soccer became a way for Tla'amin people to strive to do their best and to be the best. Sports brought out the warriors within our people, who picked up the sport and performed at an extremely high standard, with much success that could not be denied. It demonstrated we were not "less than" on the playing field. We were honouring generations of teams and players who incorporated our teachings to compete at a high standard and achieve excellence that we could strive to be part of.*

John: The teachings taught Joe to honour and recognize those who came before him and to leave the world in a better place. It is because of the work they did, including fighting or advocating for First Nations rights, that they are further ahead today than the previous generation.

Tla'amin soccer teams competed with great success in the local Powell River league, but the most important competitions they played in were up and down the coast, against other First Nations communities. Their teams played with flair but also with discipline. They used First Nations medicines and bathing. They trained hard. The players were honoured to represent their community.

SLIAMMON'S SOCCER STARS

L ESS than 100 miles north of this city is the Indian settlement of Sliammon, hard by Powell River. There the above group of young natives are establishing quite a reputation in football and baseball. Jack Lundie, former varsity soccer star, declares the three Gallagher brothers in the team are stars of the first magnitude, Joe being a full back capable of holding his own in first division circles anywhere on the coast. Top row, left to right, Dan Harry, Sam Adams, Billy Williams, Johnny Johnson, Paddy Tom, Willie Gallagher. Bottom, Charlie Bob, Jasper Francis, Alex Gallagher, Billie Charlie and Joe Gallagher.

Credit: Vancouver Sun Newspaper, Sept 30, 1925
Less than 100 miles north of this city is the Indian settlement of Sliammon, hard by Powell River. There the above group of your natives are establishing quite a reputation in football and baseball. Jack Lundle, former varsity soccer star, declares the three Gallagher brothers in the team are stars in the first magnitude. Joe being a full back more than capable of holding his own in first division circles anywhere on the coast. Top row, left to right, Dan Harry, Sam Adams, Billy Williams, Johnny Johnson, Paddy Tom, Willie Gallagher. Bottom, Charlie Bob, Jasper Francis, Alex Gallagher, Billie Charlie and Joe Gallagher.

Their teams would travel to play communities in Alert Bay, Kingcome, Campbell River, Sechelt, Musqueam and others. Later, there were native tournaments with up to 20 teams in Victoria, Duncan, and Alert Bay for both men and women. Tla'amin teams had tremendous success in native ball, playing a wide-open style that looked to be modeled after the Brazilian national team. Children looked up to the older generation of players and dreamed of playing for Tla'amin one day. Every family in the community has its soccer heroes, including the Galligos family. There were many momentous occasions for their teams reported in the press that showed this strength. (I left the spelling of Galligos as it appeared in the newspaper articles I found. There were many variations.)

1939. "Alex Louie scored a record 6 goals as the 'game's brightest star' having just returned to play his first game of the year after being away fishing. Joe, Alex and Pete Gallegos, sons of Joe and Mary, also received positive mention on their performance in this 9-0 win over their Powell River opponent."[24]

1940. "Gallagos' over-time goal puts Indians in Shield game." In another match up against Kelly Spruce the next year, "Pete Gallegos, nippy inside left, booted home the winning goal five minutes after the teams changed ends to battle out the 2-2 tie at the end of regulation time."

"It was smart headwork by his brother Joe Gallegos that paved the way for the score."[25]

1948: The Sliammon team won the league championship and cup championship. Alec Louie was the centre half and was being recruited to play on Vancouver teams.

Gallegos brothers were also on this team. "The veteran Pete Gallegos, whose bullet like drives have won the respect and admiration from visiting teams, is still an active member of the team. His two nephews, Willie and Ernie, are following in the family footsteps."

It wasn't just soccer where Mary's boys succeeded. They were excellent baseball players as well.

1929. After dominating baseball in Powell River, Joe, Willie (also known as Cooky) and Alex played for many years in Squamish in the North Shore Baseball League. In 1929, Joe Gallegos had the fourth best batting average in the league, at .398, with brother Alex in eighth place, batting 357. Willie had the second-highest pitching

---

24   Powell River News Nov. 29, 1939
25   Powell River News Feb. 29, 1940

average in the league, followed by his brother Joe in third.[26] They were dominant, to say the least.

In a 1937 article in the Powell River newspaper,[27] Lew Griffith reminisced in an old radio announcer style: "And Cooky Gallacher chucking baseballs like nobody has chucked 'em in these parts since …. And Joe poling the old apple out among the oil tanks. Man how he could hit! ... Then that time when the boys went to town in '25 and were all set to grab the BC baseball crown, only the two stars from Sliammon had to go fishing and couldn't make the date."

Joe: *I met with Les Adams and Larry Louie as part of John's and my journey. They knew my family well, so we talked a lot about my family history, but when we switched to talk about soccer, you could see and feel the excitement and energy build in the room. Soccer is a great source of pride and holds great memories.*"

John: Les and Larry had impressive individual success, each winning the Golden Boy award as the best youth soccer player in British Columbia, but more importantly they knew they were part of something that brought pride to their entire community.

Joe didn't get a chance to see Les play, but he certainly knew of his soccer prowess from his dad and the community. An article in the Powell River newspaper from Jan 13, 1954, highlighted a 7-goal performance by Les in the local men's league. The article used some of the offensive language of that day, describing a "scalping" by "redmen," but it also clearly identified Les as a player who played at a higher level than all others.

---

26   The Province newspaper Sept. 4, 1929
27   Powell River News, 1937

Les receiving Sun Tournament Golden Boy Trophy in 1955.

Joe and I both admired Larry Louie and his ability to control the ball, move quickly, and easily manage the game, all with a smile on his face. Joe was fortunate to get to play with him on multiple occasions. He played in native tournaments and for the Braves in the Powell River league. He also played for Powell River Villa in the Island Premier League. Joe learned a lot about leadership and setting the right example from Larry, using the teachings he passed on from those before him. Larry talked about Alec Louie being one of his heroes.

Both Les and Larry became inductees in the Powell River Sports Hall of Fame. Larry was recently inducted into the BC Soccer Hall of Fame.

Many others followed Larry, including Phil Galligos. Larry and Phil both worked out with the Whitecaps of the North American Soccer League. Given their level of play and natural talent, it is hard to explain why they weren't given a chance at playing games with the Whitecaps without considering racism as the reason. They more than matched the talent of some of the Canadian players on that team at the time.

Joe was determined to follow in the footsteps of the great Tla'amin soccer players, but he didn't have an easy road. He played soccer throughout his early youth with kids a school year older than him. Some of the players were almost two years older, if they happened to be born early in the year. He was born in November. He often felt bullied by his own team, which perhaps wasn't surprising, being small and knowing that being tough was how you got ahead on the reserve in those days. For the most part, he didn't get to play regularly on any of the teams he was on as a kid, but still he wanted, or maybe he needed, to be part of it. It was the only real identity he knew.

The Sliammon Braves were Joe's heroes. Soccer was at the core of their culture. It was part of the community, establishing an identity that brought pride to the community. Soccer would eventually allow Joe to feel like he belonged in Tla'amin.

1974 – Teammates

Joe: *At 13, I started playing soccer with the Powell River team that were my age. The Powell River Legion–sponsored team that John also played on. This is after my dad had told me I should quit the First Nations team I was on, because I wasn't good enough. The transition to a team from town was eased somewhat because I knew some of the players through school and baseball. It wasn't perfect, though. As the only First Nations team member, I had to figure out how to fit in with all the boys on the team. I don't know that I ever did, but at least I was on a soccer team. I didn't get to play much there, either, but I wasn't ready to quit playing soccer altogether.*

John: Even as a young teenager, Joe had become aware of feeling "different," depending on which world he was stepping into and whom he was with. Norman maintained his view about the white world around them and the importance of getting along in it. He would always say they had to be twice as good as everyone else to even be considered equal.

My first experience with First Nations soccer was a game against Joe's Coast Salish team while I was playing for a team called the Tigers. I don't remember details of the actual game, beyond seeing his entire team pile out of one old woodgrain station wagon in their green uniforms, right at the scheduled game start time.

When Joe and I started playing together on the same team at 13, he didn't get much playing time. He was quiet. We had our perceptions of Joe and the reserve, and we said things without understanding the harm. In talking about it now, he tells me he didn't really know what it was about at that age, either. He didn't really understand why things were that way, but I know now that he didn't like it.

Joe, top row, fourth from left. John, bottom row, fourth from left.

I had no understanding of the importance the game held for him. I took it seriously, but it was more important for Joe. His limited confidence off the field had led to limited confidence on the field. He always showed up, though. He wasn't going to give up.

Once we turned 16, the only playing option for us was the Powell River Men's League. Of the six teams in the league, the Braves, Sounders and Rowdies were all First Nations teams. Joe played for the Rowdies. I played at first for the high school team and then for Reg's Sporting Goods. As a small 16-year-old, I was seriously intimidated playing against each of the Sliammon teams.

The style of play in Sliammon was always fast-paced, and their use of their language and the constant chatter added to the intimidation. This was like their version of the New Zealand All Blacks doing the Haka, perhaps. They were living their identity.

Before working on this project, I characterized the Sounders and Rowdies as bullies. I reacted to a stereotype, just as I had when I first attended junior high.

Once, I was elbowed hard enough in the stomach to be winded by a Sliammon goalkeeper, but that is the only real cheap shot I ever received, in dozens of games. I received worse from other non–First Nations teams. I remember hard tackles, but I also recall being given a hand up and some shared laughter. We all played hard. That was what the game was all about.

Joe: *I wouldn't say anyone ever deserves to be elbowed in the stomach, including John, but it isn't like he was all that innocent. Sure, we all played hard, but in his case, he also played on the edge. He was like a soccer version of Brad Marchand. He had talent, he scored goals, he was relatively small, but he also had sharp elbows, and had the ability to draw penalties. He also never stopped talking!*

John: This made me laugh when Joe shared it with me, but there was a serious side to it as well. Even in my soccer experience, I was holding First Nations players to a different standard.

My last experience with First Nations soccer in Powell River was as a referee. Joe was living in Victoria at that point. I was back in Powell River for the weekend, and I ran into our old coach Jim McNeil, who was responsible for supplying referees for Men's League games. He asked me if I could ref a game between the Sounders and the Rowdies. Jim had been so good to us, so I couldn't say no, despite my apprehension. There I was, an experienced player but not an experienced referee, as the only non–First Nations person at the pitch, ready to call a game between two fast teams, with no linesmen. There was a good crowd that were more than happy to let me know how I was doing. I had talked to the two team captains at the start of the game and let them both know it was going to be a challenge with no linesmen, but I would give it a go. That didn't stop the players from grumbling all game long about offside calls, and non-offside calls. They may have been right. The game was close, so by the end I was hearing plenty of objections from the crowd. As the clock was running out, I started to think about how I was going to get to my car quickly after the game.

When I blew the final whistle and started to walk off, players ran up to me with handshakes and thanks for coming out, from both teams. Once again, I had been caught up in my own preconceptions.

1978 – Hawaii – Work ethic

Joe: *At different stages in my life, I became ready for and accepting of certain teachings. As I got older, I gained more appreciation for them and would seek them out. It wasn't really until I was in Grade 11, a year before I would be heading off to university, that I became exposed to and open to listening to the people around me that were sharing teachings.*

John: Joe was learning about Tla'amin culture through soccer. He started playing with the men in Tla'amin, and he would hear stories about how the older players would train. He was listening to players like Larry Louie, Alvin Wilson, and Jackie Timothy as they provided him with teachings he could carry with him. Soccer provided the framework by which he was able to start learning and growing. These lessons shaped the kind of player he was, and more importantly, the person he became. Teachings are the truths that guide the Tla'amin people and have enabled them to thrive and survive.

Joe picked up little pieces of the language and other teachings. They used Tla'amin language on the field, including:

Mey hay – In the middle

Quot/kwot – Leave it

Peh pie ye – You're by yourself

When the Sliammon Braves were invited to play in a tournament in Hawaii, Joe's Aunt Mia did the kindest thing for him. She convinced Norman that Joe should go on that trip. He went with the view that he was going to play, and he trained hard to be ready. Though he was disappointed not to get on the field, he still views this as a life-changing trip. At 16, Joe was the youngest on the team. He was far from home, away from his parents, and watching the other players on the team. It helped him realize that he wanted to go to university away from Tla'amin, and that playing university soccer was his number one priority. He was driven to train. He went at it hard every day at that point, using what he had learned from the trip to Hawaii.

There is a traditional medicine made from Devil's Club that is ground into a powder. Coast Salish athletes would bathe in the river and hit themselves with cedar boughs to the point of making their skin red, and then they would rub the powder in to strengthen muscles and even heal strains and sprains. When Joe was older and playing at home, the guys on the team would help him understand the teachings behind these practices. He learned the most from talking to Jackie Timothy. The Timothy family had great soccer players. Jackie was also a carver and an artist with a lot of great knowledge that he shared with Joe.

Pre-colonization, First Nations people needed to work hard. They were continually preparing for the future. If they didn't, they wouldn't survive. They shared with each other. They would use various techniques to catch salmon depending on the time of year, and they would gather clams, catch herring, hunt for deer and fowl, and gather plants and berries.

Colonization robbed them of much of their work ethic by isolating and restricting First Nations and damaging their traditional territory. They were a ward of the government; they were no longer looking after themselves. The traditional teachings explain the importance of building a strong body, mind, and spirit. They advise people to take care of themselves. Like the warriors who came before them, as soccer players the young men needed to do the hard work. Soccer became a way of turning them back into warriors.

When he was younger, Joe would see the generation of soccer players before him arrive home in a crummy (logging transport) after a long day of work and immediately head out to play soccer until dark. His people had that commitment and vitality. There was always discussion about being the strongest you could be. There is a word for this: *tklaasum*, which means to be strong and solidly built.

Norman's strictness went back to traditional teachings on hard work and discipline, which he instilled in Joe. Joe has worked hard throughout his life, but it started in sports. It almost got to the point where it wasn't just a game; It was his life. Soccer was a game he learned to love, but at the beginning it was about survival.

His training before going to the University of Victoria had him getting up every morning and going for a run, and then bathing in the river. He was building his hunger to play. He was listening to what other people were telling him. Based on the teachings, he was cleansing himself and keeping his spirit strong. The spirit bath is done in running water; you dunk yourself four times and acknowledge the purpose of being there. You let things go that are heavy and bothering you; you come away rejuvenated. This wasn't just physical training. It was purposeful. It was holistic. Soccer gave Joe a reason to follow this tradition. He's not sure he would have found it any other way.

* * *

1979 – UVic Tryouts – **Be a hawk**

Knowledge Keeper Sulksun explained the difference between a hawk and an eagle. Hawks are very deliberate hunters. They are looking for the right opportunity, and when they find it, they strike on it. An eagle is an interesting bird because it will eat dead things. The hawk won't. It will only eat something that is fresh on the bone. We want to have a hawk's attitude of making and taking the opportunity to be successful. You need to go after what you want. Joe is a hawk.

Joe and I were still trying to find our way around residence at UVic and get familiar with all the amenities, including the gym and workout facilities that were available to us. Eventually we made it to the sports fields. There seemed to be as many fields there as in all of Powell River. The UVic soccer teams were practicing. Joe told me he was going to see about getting a tryout. I gave him credit for wanting to try, but I didn't think he had a hope. I was worried for him, thinking he would be disappointed at not making the team. This shows how little I knew. Joe knew what he wanted and went after it. I hadn't understood the extent of the training Joe had undertaken before heading to UVic.

Compared to what he knew growing up, he felt no fear in approaching the UVic coaches. He somehow felt it was what he was meant to do. The worst thing they could say was no, and there had already been so many "no's" in his life that it didn't seem another would matter. He didn't have a plan B if they did say no. He felt supported by a combination of his history, not knowing any better, the fact that he had been training hard, and this newfound freedom, being away from home. He felt empowered.

Joe chose UVic for university because it was smaller than UBC, and he thought that would give him a better chance to make the soccer team. Apparently, he was just stubborn enough to think he could make it, despite not getting a lot of playing time on the Powell River Legion–sponsored team or the Max Cameron High School team.

Joe had never been a starter on any of the teams he had played on, yet as a walk-on he became a starter early in the season with the

Junior Varsity Norsemen. He was playing centre midfield and scoring almost every game. He became known for his powerful shot, earning the nickname Thunderfoot from the JV Coach. Later, when playing in Native Ball tournaments with other native players, he was given the nickname Smoke. Joe must have inherited this ability from his Great Uncle Pete Galligos, who was known for his own thundering shot.

Early on, the JV Norsemen played a game against Mount Doug School, a school that both the JV coach, George Smith, and Varsity coach Brian Hughes had sons playing for. The JV team went on to win, and Joe scored three goals. That was one of the last times he played for the junior team. He was moved up to the Vikes, the varsity team. He played his initial game for them at Topaz Park in Victoria. This game for the senior team occurred before he turned 18, which was a real point of pride, and took place less than four years after his dad had told him he was too slow and no good, and that he should just quit playing soccer.

Early 1980s - Anger – **Manage your fear**

Joe: *As a young boy and as teenager, fear was paralyzing to me. It came from many sources, both inside the home I was living in, the reserve I grew up on, and the racist society around the reserve. It made me feel alone all the time. Being able to work through my fear was a turning point in my life, but it was the hardest thing to do.*

Les Adams told Joe a story explaining what it meant to manage fear.

Les spotted a bear on his Tla'amin property. This was concerning, as he had grandchildren who would play in his yard. He had things to do, so he asked someone else to take care of it for him. When he got home, he learned that this other person had called the conservation service to tell them they had a bear. This, to Les, was not taking care of it, so when he saw the bear again, he shot it. He didn't like killing the bear, but he was protecting his grandchildren.

Shortly afterwards, a conservation officer called, and said, "I understand you have a bear problem."

"Not anymore. I shot him."

The conservation officer said, "You can get in a lot of trouble for shooting a bear."

Les, always quick with a response, said: "Not as much trouble as I can get in for shooting a conservation officer."

Les just felt he needed to do what he needed to do and approached the solution without fear.

It would be ignorant to not fear the bear, but he still needed to respect and understand it, so he could move ahead with courage. He didn't want to kill the bear, but he needed to do what he needed to do.

There was so much fear in their community, much of it going back to colonization, which resulted in dysfunction that led to lateral violence and bullying. This was in addition to the racism they had to deal with. Joe lived with fear for the first 15 years or more of his life.

In soccer, you can't play with fear. You are a better person and a better player when you control your emotions.

Alex Louie, star of Sliammon Soccer in the '30s and '40s, used to help out on teams Joe was on. He wasn't a coach, but he was there helping. He'd give them a rubdown after the game with hands that were still strong, and he would pass on stories. Joe was 22 or 23 and playing in a tournament in Alert Bay. These were highly competitive tournaments, and emotions ran high. Joe would get angry back then. Alex told him, "You're not a dog. Only dogs get mad out there." He gave him teachings about leadership.

It wasn't soccer that Joe was mad about. His life was tough, and in his early twenties he was trying to figure out who he was and where he belonged. Soccer became an avenue to vent. His anger was a way for him to avoid addressing his fear.

When Joe played for non-Sliammon teams, he wasn't angry. It only came out when playing for Sliammon. Those matches were important. Even when playing in big games for UVic, it was different. There, he was playing for a uniform. When he was playing for Sliammon teams, he was playing for his community, and his family. He was playing for pride.

He was more numb than angry when it came to life outside of Tla'amin. Soccer helped him build confidence, strength, and resilience. He was finally able to make his own choices when he got to UVic. There was so much fear in his life, growing up in Norman's house, Tla'amin and Powell River. He didn't feel safe anywhere. So much violence and anger. He needed to find something else. This was the beginning of him no longer being afraid.

Joe took this lesson into his work. In one of the interviews I had with Cynthia Johansen, CEO of the BC Registrar of Nurses, she commented on Joe's lack of fight-or-flight response. He was able to patiently work through very difficult issues without banging on the table or retreating.

1980–1981 – Most Improved Player Awards - Be your best

Joe: *Our Knowledge Keepers always spoke about the importance of doing your best and being your best. For me, contrary to the efforts and impacts of settler colonialism to keep our First Nations peoples down, I understood this teaching first from the stories of my great uncles and other Tla'amin athletes who excelled in soccer and baseball in the early 1900s onward. Their excellence, from being at their best, couldn't be denied, as gifted First Nations athletes who applied our First Nations methods to train and take care of their bodies were enabled to perform at an elite level. This was passed on to me as I continued to play soccer and learn from the great Sliammon men's teams, from the age of 16 onward. It was a roadmap to strive to be my best as a Sliammon athlete. It was the positive Tla'amin identity I had to have. It was also the answer to the challenge my dad constantly stated, about having to be twice as good as the white people at what you do if you are to make it in this world. We are taught to be our best, and we need that to survive settler colonialism.*

John: Joe returned home as soon as his first year at UVic ended and missed the wrap-up dinner for the Vikes. He was pleasantly surprised when he returned to school in September to discover he had won the award as most improved player. It was even more amazing when he won the same trophy the following year.

Winning the most improved player award two years in a row illustrates a trait that has followed Joe throughout his life. He is never satisfied with last year's performance.

Here he was, a player who couldn't make the team in high school, becoming the guy getting awards. He had never worked as hard as he did then, and he was so buoyed by his newfound freedom, away from home and the many challenges that came in that Tla'amin/Powell River environment. There are two words that Knowledge Keeper Sulksun uses from his hən̓q̓əmin̓əm̓ Coast Salish language: *yukwithit*, which roughly translates into English as "free yourself," and *tiimithit*, which means "be your best." That's how he felt at UVic. He was free, and that provided the opportunity for him to be at his best. He wonders what would have become of him if he didn't make that team, though. Soccer was the only Tla'amin identity he understood at the time.

UVIC Varsity Soccer 1982. Joe front row, second from left.

He was establishing himself as a UVic soccer player and was gaining more and more confidence. He was enjoying his successes and reading about them in highly positive stories in the school's newspaper. Being the humble man he is, he also felt awkward about it.

In a game against the Victoria Athletics—a top team in the Vancouver Island Premier League—he had a free-kick outside the 18-yard line. It was a close game; his teammate said to him "Don't miss." Like he needed to hear that.

"I won't! Just roll me the f'ing ball."

He just hammered it. He knew he could do it. He had no doubt. Everyone knew he was taking the shot and he still scored. His confidence was growing.

Joe saw UVic soccer as a gift. He was able to train five days a week and play one or two games on the weekend. The university had great facilities. He was in the gym working out. The team had trainers working with them. He was doing all the things he could to become a better player.

He was a long way removed from the slightly chunky 135 pounds he weighed at 14. At 18, he was 155 pounds of muscle; he was fast, he was strong, he tackled hard, and more than held his own. He was doing things to make the team successful.

He was living the dream. There was always a political side to it, but for Joe it was like being a professional. He got to play every day. He was flying on planes to play in other cities, traveling in a group in their team sweaters. They received brand-new uniforms every year, and he received a scholarship to buy new boots. At first it was $500, then it became $1,000 a year to play soccer. It was awesome. He played in Montreal, Toronto, Ottawa, and other cities. While they were in Ottawa, they played against Carleton University. Later, when he was working in health, he drove by the university campus on the way to meetings and recognized the field, which brought back great memories.

During his time with UVic soccer, they made it to the intercollegiate Canadian championship game one year, and the semis in another. They won the Jackson Cup as the top team in the Vancouver Island Premier League one year as well. They were consistently in the top three on Vancouver Island.

It wasn't until he was playing university soccer that he really started thinking about who he was. He didn't think he belonged in the First Nations world, and he was academically advanced, but he didn't know if he belonged at university. He saw himself through the lens of his soccer identity, and beyond that, the world was confusing.

UVic soccer helped Joe create an identity. Going home, he was able to develop a sense of really belonging to something, thanks to soccer. He started representing the community. He was able to contribute. He had an appetite for the game, and he couldn't get enough of it. He had come out of a world where he felt trapped, and now he was free, and he was holding on to an identity that he never knew he could achieve.

Joe didn't have the same appetite for school as he did for soccer. He and I took a Canadian History class in first year. It was challenging enough, being an 8:30 Monday morning class. What made it even more difficult was recognizing it wasn't *his* history. Joe and I laugh now, recognizing 40 years later that we are finally really learning Canadian history. At UVic, there was barely a mention of First Nations.

Joe also struggled with calculus, which was strange given that math was one of his best subjects in high school. It wasn't an ability issue. Going to class just wasn't a priority. Soccer was the thing keeping him at university, at least long enough to get a degree.

Even though Joe found playing soccer at UVic transformational, he never really felt he was part of the university community. It wasn't hard to see and feel the racism in men's soccer back then. In one game against UBC, the coach was upset about something, and he referred to Joe with a racist comment—as though that had something to do with whatever was happening on the field. As a First Nations person, the culmination of such micro-aggressions really stung Joe. They were ongoing reminders that he did not fit in with the privileged class.

When such acts of racism happened to him back then, he didn't know what to do with them. He didn't feel he had any power to do anything other than pile it on himself with all the other incidents. Today, when he runs into someone who is racist and doesn't understand or isn't willing to be part of the truth and reconciliation process, he likes to borrow a quote that the late Leonard George shared with him.

"We are all born ignorant, but one must work hard to remain stupid."

Joe: *I was just 17 years old when I first went away to university. At that time, it was a chance to get away from the challenging life at home and on the reserve and be part of the bigger world. My grades in high school were good and enabled me to be accepted into the University of Victoria. My main interest was to play soccer at university. To be free to fulfil my aspiration to be a Tla'amin soccer player. I also thought I was escaping all the trauma, but I wasn't. I just was physically away from my family, the reserve, and the community of Powell River for a while and not dealing with any of the intergenerational trauma I had experienced while living there. My parents' experience with residential schools and other negative influences had shaped their lives and the lives of others in my family and community members. I know it is real, and as I continue to unpack it even today, I still have a hard time expressing the impact that it has had. It took me a long time to start feeling good about myself. I am still working on it."*

John: While hearing Joe tell his history, I kept coming back to the question of what happened that allowed Joe to make the phenomenal transformation he has in his life. How did he become a leader on the soccer field and the founding CEO of the largest First Nations institution in the country? Where did this fire come from?

I was introduced by Joe to Sulksun (Shane Point), a Coast Salish Knowledge Keeper who explained his understanding of Joe's transformation.

Sulksun: "Some of our people actually go and look for their gift. There are mechanisms within our families and communities to do that. When I think about Joe, specifically him, I don't think he was looking for that gift, but it found him. It found him after the transition from Powell River/Sliammon to Victoria. In that transition period in Victoria, the gift found him. Of course, it builds up over time. Joe's genius constantly amazes me.

"We often look for one thing that makes the change, but I think, in terms of myself and others that I've seen in my lifetime, is that it's a combination of things. So, when you think about Joe Gallagher and his time frame—the time his father and mom grew up in—your understanding of an Indian reserve is that it's a village with relatives, and people as a support system. But really what it is, is a place of restriction. You can't come off the reserve. Up to the 1960s, you couldn't come off without permission from an Indian agent.

"Geography and ecosystems dictate beliefs, values, and language. His background from his mom and dad, the village that he grew up in, is all a part of the mix. When you think about Sliammon, it's isolated from Powell River. You have that racism that's happening at that place, in that time, as well. So, I believe that part of Joe's awakening to his vast intelligence and his ability to see, not just right now but a hundred and forty years into the future, and what that looks like, comes from a combination [of ways] of becoming free.

"So, going to school in Powell River, his vast intelligence is there—it just hasn't awakened. Moving off reserve, moving to Victoria to go to school, is his awakening. It's those states becoming unrestricted. His growth at university happens because he's free. The thought of freedom doesn't come in a moment. ... Moving away from home, moving away from family, going into an entirely new environment, a new social system, and in the end the new place—a new geography. I think that that combination of things woke that gift up, or that gift found him. "

Janene Erickson—Nak'azdli Whut'en—of FNHA added her perspective.

"You know he is gifted [from] the way that he spoke, and what I saw of him. As I learned more of his story, about his family life and experiences, it just makes sense.

"A reflection of the trauma our people have received is [that] we are not acknowledging or understanding the spiritual element of our lives, and as holistic people it was a strong component of who we were. It's not really talked about, but there was spiritual abuse that occurred through the Church. I've heard from Elders that have solidified that understanding for me, that losing our connection to our creator is one of our greatest traumas.

"Some of the teachings say that people are given gifts. Everyone has a unique gift that they bring, or they foster. There's not one person that has it all, so we need to work together. The whole point of our lives is trying to figure out how to be good to one another and to be generous with one another, and to be kind and compassionate.

"Joe knows who he is. He knows what he can offer. He knows his strengths and is not threatened by people. He brings people up to work at his level."

John: When Joe went off to university, he was able to free himself and to begin being who he was meant to be—both a skilled athlete and a visionary leader.

In those days, he was one of the few Tla'amin students who completed university. It is far more common today. After being in school, he felt he needed to reconnect with his community to better understand himself and to develop his gift. He was living in two worlds and was not sure if he fit in either of them.

He applied to the Master of Public Administration program at UVic but was denied because his GPA was a fraction of a point below the stated requirement. This was frustrating because he got one bad grade in a third-year course called "Leadership Methods for Recreation." There was no one to advocate for him to continue his education, as there is in place today.

After that, he just wanted to be at home. It was what he knew. When he did reconnect with his community, it felt almost like exhaling. He was Tla'amin. He felt he needed to have that connection, but he also needed to better understand who he was.

He still has a need, every once and a while, to go home and try to reconnect and see where things stand. One of the characteristics of being a First Nations person is having a deep connection with the land and territory—which is one reason the unceded territory acknowledgement is so important.

Territory, in this case, is much larger than the Tla'amin reserve. The Coast Salish traditionally traveled a lot, as a community and families, so they have relatives in Sechelt, Squamish, North Vancouver, Victoria, Musqueam and the Fraser River, for the salmon fishery. Because he has all these connections, Joe has always lived in Coast Salish territory.

His people always moved around; it was a colonial choice to keep them on reserves, to stop them from traveling. They have a special bond to their territory. But under colonialism, they were confined. It wasn't just the residential schools that brought dysfunction.

Joe has a special bond to Tla'amin. When his son was born, Joe buried the stump of his umbilical cord at home, based on one of the few teachings he received from his dad. He is starting to pick some of these traditions up as he gets older.

1980s – Bringing his knowledge to Tla'amin – **Trust in team**

Joe: *For the soccer team to be successful, everyone needs to believe in everyone else. Everyone must do the work to get ready for the big game, and once on the field everyone has a role to play and must be able to count on one another to pull their weight and perform at a* *high level—to do their best. It is the same for our organizations and nations. However, things are often not this way for many First Nations today, because the system imposed on them by settler colonialism is not based on First Nations teachings. Settler colonialism is based on Western, patriarchal, Christian, capitalistic, and imposed systems that create divisions among our people. After a hundred and fifty years or more of this, much mistrust has been created among our peoples.*

You build trust in a team from everyone doing their best, in a structure where everyone focuses on their role. Everything is relational—connected. Everyone needs to do the hard work and avoid letting others down.

It's more than just going out there when the whistle blows. It takes uniforms, preparation, rides to get everyone to the field. It takes a common mindset, philosophies, and values. The team members all need to support each other—to be part of the community.

If you pass the ball to someone who is not at their best, then your team is not at their best. To succeed, you must believe in one another. You need to trust everyone to play their position, and they must trust you to play yours.

Joe's UVic degree was in Leisure Studies. He would tell people he was taking Recreational Admin, because he felt the term "Leisure Studies" would not be taken seriously. It turned out to be an excellent degree, and the education he received has served him well.

Joe talks about the time it took for him to complete his degree and tends to downplay the accomplishment. In my case, following two years of school in Victoria, I moved to Vancouver for a summer job at MacMillan Bloedel and ended up staying there for nine years. I got a job in the accounting department and went through the CGA program, which is now known as Chartered Professional Accountant, or CPA. At the time, I felt I wanted to get on with life and was happy to get a paycheque, but I regret not finishing university.

This could have caused issues for me later in my career, because every senior-level job I held had a university degree as a base requirement. I never hid my lack of one from anyone, but no one ever asked, either. This was simply another unearned advantage I received.

Joe's Leisure Studies degree program had a co-op component. He was running behind and needed to get his degree on track, so the university was good enough to allow him to do back-to-back co-op terms. They were also good enough to allow him to do them at home in Tla'amin.

He ran recreational programs and did education coordinator work with kids in the community, which he loved. As part of his co-op program, he was also able to establish the Sliammon Soccer Club. He was learning that he could contribute positively to his community.

He had established some great relationships playing for UVic in the Vancouver Island Premier League, and with help from them and others from the community, they were able to get their Sliammon soccer team directly into the top division.

Joe met George Smith when he was the junior varsity soccer coach at UVic, after Joe first walked onto the team. George was good to him even when he moved up to the varsity team, the Vikes. Joe was living in UVic residence, and George would come by and pick him up and bring him home for breakfast before games.

In addition to his coaching duties, George was president of the Vancouver Island Soccer league. Joe reached out to him when he heard that the league was being split into northern and southern divisions. The north included teams from Powell River, Port Alberni, Nanaimo, and Campbell River. Joe let George know there were many great soccer players back home, and many were better than he was. George trusted Joe and presented the proposal on their behalf to enter a team into the league, which was approved. The Tla'amin Soccer Club played in the Premier League for two years.

Having their club granted premier league status didn't sit well with everyone, in particular the Powell River Villa club. Back when Villa joined the Vancouver Island Soccer Association, they had had to start in a lower division and work their way up. They felt the Sliammon club should do the same. Maybe some on Villa just knew how good they were.

A group, led by Joe, had to support the team, and not just the team on the field. He was supporting fundraising efforts and driving the team van to get them to games on Vancouver Island. He would load up his bag with extra shin pads, tape, and other items someone might need, because someone always needed something. His felt it was important to help take care of others and encourage them to take care of themselves, particularly the younger players on the team. Joe wanted to demonstrate this, so they would be the next to step up.

The first time the Sliammon club played Powell River Villa in the Premier League, Joe's team was nervous, and they got off to a slow start, giving up an early goal. But after they settled in, the team's talent shone through, and they ended up winning the game 5-2, with a big crowd from Tla'amin spurring them on. It was a big win for the community, and their most satisfying victory of the season.

Credit: Glacier Publishing – 1984 Sliammon FC vs Villa FC. Joe scoring.

Most of the time, their people were treated as "less than," but on the soccer field they were equal. It was a symbolic moment. Like many Tla'amin teams before them, this one more than showed that they belonged in a part of the world that otherwise didn't welcome them. It is notable that the Powell River newspaper article about this game did not have the disrespectful tone writers had used for Sliammon teams from prior generations. No reference to "scalping" or "redmen." The article was positive about the Sliammon team, saying the win came in "fine style." Joe, the spokesperson for the team, was quoted numerous times in the article, including the comment that "it was our most satisfying win of the season."

Unfortunately, the Sliammon Soccer Club only lasted two seasons. Joe had to leave before the end of season one to go back to Victoria and finish his degree, and the team got hit by some unfortunate community Indian Act politics.

While starting up the Premier League team, Joe was also trying to build bridges between the First Nations and non–First Nations communities—between Tla'amin and Powell River. That wasn't something that could happen overnight, but he wanted everyone to keep their focus there. To this aim, Joe set up a seven-a-side soccer tournament, along with Calvin Harry. Joe had played in one in Victoria and really enjoyed the format.

In the first year of the tournament, Joe entered a team with his brother and a mix of community folks and players from town—both First Nations and white guys. They ended up playing in the final and winning, but most important to Joe was that they create some balance and build a small bridge to more positive relations between Tla'amin players and the white players from town. It was a success in that regard, as the tournament became an annual event. Calvin ran it long enough for Joe's son, Ben, to eventually play in it.

* * *

Post UVic

Joe: *Too many times, I was the only Indian in a situation, whether it be in a school classroom or on a sports field. I got good at biting my tongue just to avoid the fight, ignore the slur, and be numb to the racism in my life. This has continued pretty much for my whole life and well into adulthood. As I grew into a man, the fear and shame that was instilled in me from growing up on the reserve dissipated. It has not gone away. When I was getting close to finishing my degree at UVic, I was very aware that I really didn't belong in the white world. I had developed a lot as a soccer player and had moved towards living my Tla'amin soccer player identity, which I took great pride in. I realized I needed to go home to stay connected to my community, to be with my people. As a young man going back, it was going to be different for me, as I was old enough to begin to understand why things were the way they were and to determine what I wanted my life to be like moving forward.*

John: When Joe finished his degree at UVic and moved to Vancouver, he played with the NorVan team in the Vancouver Metro Premier League. He also played with the Victoria Athletics as he found himself moving between Vancouver, Victoria and Tla'amin in the '80s.

He moved back home in 1990 to do some community work, and at that time joined the Villa soccer team. He didn't want to play in the local men's league. He belonged in the Premier League, but still, he joined Villa with some trepidation.

A lot of guys in his community warned him against playing for them, saying, "They won't treat you well." They had experienced their own share of unfair and prejudiced treatment. But he still wanted to play. He played every game, and they had a very successful season, winning the Jackson Cup as champions of the Island League. With that victory, they moved on to the provincial playoffs with their first match against Joe's old team, NorVan.

For some reason, he never got off the bench in that game. Not in regulation, not when it went to overtime, and not for the penalty kicks that NorVan won to settle the game. After that game, the NorVan guys came up to Joe and asked him if he was injured or something. They couldn't believe he didn't play. He couldn't either, although he kept that to himself at the time. They had chosen to play guys that were like them. Those they also knew off the field. White guys.

Joe had earned a place on a number of good teams. He was part of Jackson Cup–winning teams with UVic, Victoria Athletics and PR Villa. Soccer had taught Joe how to be a good teammate with people from other cultures. They had a common goal as a team. Looking back, Joe wonders how they perceived him as a teammate. If he helped them win, if he did his best, if they could count on him as reliable, did he hold up his part of the bargain? I am sure he did. Doing so is simply part of his identity.

Joe didn't attend the end-of--season wrapup for Villa, but the day after, one of the good guys came by his house and gave him the Rookie of the Year trophy. He didn't know what to say. He couldn't get over the fact that he had played all season, yet didn't play the most important game of the year. I guess Norman was right. He had to be twice as good.

April 1, 1940 – "Much Controversy Over Soccer All-Stars" Powell River News article by Dawson Pirie

The article discusses the selection of an all-star team from Powell River being put together to take on a team from West Vancouver, and a few controversies over who was selected. The only name specifically mentioned was Stan Harry of the Sliammon Braves, who was a hard worker, but the "little redskin still has a lot to learn about playing …". Instead, some of the "older players" were selected for the team. Was Stan's not being allowed to play foreshadowing something that would happen to many others—including Joe, 50 years later?

Joe wonders whether, if he had stayed in Powell River, he would have played another year for Villa. He probably would have. It wasn't the first time he had experienced frustration like that, and it wouldn't be the last. He certainly would have wanted to be in the Premier League. He didn't have to make that decision, however, because he was on his way back to Victoria.

*   *   *

Joe also participated in soccer in other ways during the '80s. In Victoria, he got involved in futsal , an indoor version of soccer played with a small, hard ball. One thing led to another, and his team ended up having a challenge match with an Indigenous team from Australia.

Futsal was just beginning to grow in Canada, with its early origins in greater Vancouver and Victoria. Joe loved it. Next thing he knew, he was playing in the 1988 World Cup of Futsal, representing Canada along with a couple of other First Nations guys and others from the Premier League in Greater Vancouver. It was a round-robin tournament in Australia against Paraguay, Portugal, and England. In their first two matches, they rarely had possession. Their opposition had the game down to another level and pace. They did manage to tie England, and Joe scored a goal. Another great experience. Joe was the only player from Tla'amin, and he was proud to represent Tla'amin Nation.

Team Canada playing Futsol in Australia, 1988. Joe bottom left. This tournament was clearly a big deal. Look who else is on the marquis.

*　　*　　*

16. Native Soccer

Joe: *Playing Native Soccer and playing for the Sliammon soccer teams was the best! Our native tournaments were incredibly competitive, with bragging rights on the line. It was a chance to follow in the footsteps of all my great Sliammon soccer idols who came before me and do the community proud. It also provided an opportunity to play against and with many great First Nations soccer players from other nations, many of whom I have a special connection with today.*

Sliammon Masters. Joe top row, fourth from left.

I had the great fortune, when I was in Victoria, to be involved with some folks who were very appreciative of Native Soccer players. Many of them were referees in the Island Premier League. There were a select few who also refereed in many First Nations tournaments, including the very large one that took place in Victoria every year around Easter.

These refs ended up getting involved and organized what became the first international trip of the Native Indian Football Association (NIFA) in 1990. A select team of players from BC First Nations communities, including Joe, was created, and they travelled to England.

Max Low, in the Victoria Times-Colonist on May 2, 1990, quoted referee Graham Cope, born in England, as one of the referees who wanted to show off the talent of First Nations soccer players: "I got involved with refereeing at a lot of Indian Tournaments and have been impressed by their talents. I think we can go to England and show them some pretty good soccer."

Again, Joe was the only one from Tla'amin. It was great for him to get to know players from other First Nations and travel all over the world with them—and play a lot of soccer. Dano Thorne, Coast Salish from Cowichan, was on that trip. Joe had played with and against him In Native ball since the early 1980s. Dano later picked up the reins of the NIFA. He was a skilled player who won many team and individual awards as a player. Thanks to his deep passion for the game, he remains a driving force for Native Soccer as a coach. Among his many successes, he recently coached the Women's Canadian team to the gold medal at the 2015 and 2017 World Indigenous Games. Like Joe, his support of First Nations goes well beyond the playing field, and he has used his leadership skills and passion for sports to improve First Nations wellness. Joe and Dano remain good friends today.

Dano Thorne, Larry Louie, and Joe at BC Soccer Event 2022

Joe back row, second from right. Team that travelled to England, 1991

On that inaugural trip, they played four games in England, and Joe was impressed, seeing the passion the English players had for the game. Every tackle was played as though it would be the last they would ever make. The First Nations team was high on skill, but it took them some time to adjust and match their opponents' aggression. They played a mix of pro and semi-pro teams around Stoke-On-Trent, which is where they stayed, and they did manage to win their last game.

At this point in his life, Joe had played a lot of soccer on some great teams and learned many lessons from each of them. It was now the early '90s, and he had started to dedicate himself more to his consulting work. He recognized that he needed to start thinking about establishing a career, getting married and having kids. He wanted to start applying more of what he had learned. The game couldn't be his priority forever, though he wasn't ready to give it up yet.

University soccer had kept him in Victoria, but he didn't feel he belonged in the non–First Nations world. When he went home and totally immersed himself in that world, that was also difficult. He wanted to move faster; to be more progressive. He felt there was a different way to look at things, so he decided to plant a foot in each world, returning eventually to Vancouver. He also wanted more access to sports, social activities, and career opportunities.

At one point, he did try out for a first division team in North Vancouver after he was done playing in the Premier League. He arranged to join them, and after a couple of practices he played for them in a preseason tournament at Ambleside Park. They had no idea who or what to expect.

On arrival, the team manager dug to the bottom of his box of jerseys and pulled out number 22. For those not familiar, a lower number is typically given to those players expected to have serious playing time. He didn't play the first half of the first game, which was fair enough, given they hadn't seen his play. Then he came out in the second half and scored two goals. After the game, the manager traded his 22 for a 14. Joe's saving grace in soccer was that he could always hit the ball with pace. It was a great way to get people to take notice. He still had it.

He played some over-30s soccer, but he was starting to suffer from injuries. It was bound to happen, with the amount of playing he had done. He had his first knee surgery in 1996, and that was followed by two more. He was slowing down.

His move to Vancouver was also for practical reasons. His work required a lot of travel to various places. Being based in Tla'amin meant being stuck away from home a lot more than you would living in Vancouver. But he still commuted back and forth between Vancouver and Tla'amin as needed.

Humility

Joe: *If you think you are good at something, it is not for you to tell everyone. Our teaching taught us to be humble. Not to boast or brag. We are to be strong, be confident, but not arrogant. Be generous and kind and have gratitude for all the gifts that we have been given. Most important is that we must always be open to learning more, as there are so many things we don't know. The quality of our character was important. In addition to all this, you always need to pick up after yourself. No job is too big or too small.*

John: First Nations teachings focus on humility, which has been challenged by the form of government that was imposed on them. They were moved into a hierarchical system that tests the ability to have humble leaders. We certainly see the lack of humility in non–First Nations political organizations, so it's no surprise this has affected First Nations as well.

A crucial aspect of humility teachings is that the First Nations worldview starts with the land, then the plants and animals, and finally the people. The people have a responsibility to take care of all things for future generations.

Leadership is not about grabbing power. It is about taking responsibility. Leaders have the responsibility to share knowledge, authority, and wealth.

It took me searching old newspaper articles to learn the degree to which Joe was respected as a soccer player. He was too humble to speak of this. From the Victoria Times-Colonist, March 31, 1986: "Sliammon Midfielder Joe Gallagher, a former University of Victoria star, who had a hand in setting up several of the goals in the final, was named the tournament's outstanding player." This was at the Totem Tournament, played in Victoria on Easter weekend every year. The most important tournament of the year in Native ball.

Leave the team in a better place

Joe: *First Nations were taught that we are given responsibility to take care of this place and these things for future generations. It's a system we would grow up with, benefit from, and give back to. We are stewards of the land. Thriving, it sustains us. If we leave it in a worse place for future generations, we have done it all wrong. This applies to everything we do. In today's context, we must work to dismantle settler colonialism and to address all of its harmful impacts. We continue to strive to have our rights and title recognized and to establish our rightful place in relation to our territories, and within society. We continue to figure out how to build a better world for our children. To leave the world in a better place for future generations."*

John: It is the same with the health work, and with the teams Joe played on. The players wanted to be part of a team the community was proud of. They wanted to build a team that young kids wanted to be part of. They wanted to leave the team in a good place, so future generations would feel its honour and want to continue the legacy.

Playing soccer was great for Joe. His identity as a person from Tla'amin was formed through soccer. He learned some of his history, culture, and teachings. He would spend more time after that paying it forward.

He coached kids in Tla'amin, and he built programs to challenge people, like the seven-a-side tournament. He coached the UVic women's soccer team for a year, which was a lot of fun. He was able to share his knowledge, the team improved, and he worked with great people. He even coached baseball one year. They weren't a particularly good team, as not many players had any previous experience. It was great.

Later, he moved on to coach his son's soccer teams, but Ben's real passion was lacrosse. Like Joe, he was born in November, so he was a younger member of the team as well. In his early years of lacrosse, for a long time he didn't get to play much. Joe was frustrated by this, because he could see he wasn't being treated fairly, but Ben would never give up. Joe isn't sure that there was any prejudice involved, but there was certainly favouritism. Ben wasn't going to get any better if he didn't play.

Joe supported his son as much as he could. He recognized how hard it can be for a kid trying to play sports. Joe was often surprised that Ben kept wanting to play, because he would come home so frustrated that the coach wouldn't give him a fair shake. But he kept at it. He would practice on his own, sometimes with Joe, but mostly with friends. When Joe played catch with him, he used a baseball glove and threw the ball back to him, lacking proficiency with a lacrosse stick. Ben stuck with it and developed into a good lacrosse player, playing Junior B and at university. His passion was very familiar to Joe.

Joe was proud of Ben as a lacrosse player in many ways, including his willingness to referee games for younger kids. They needed refs to be able to play. Both recognized that with sport, you become part of a community, and you need to give back as best you can.

Part 5

URBAN EXPOSURE AND UNDERSTANDING

17. Alternate School

Joe: *Beyond the residential school system, Indigenous-specific racism in the public education system is systemic and results in poor education outcomes for First Nations students compared with the rest of the student population. In too many situations, First Nations students are deemed difficult, for a variety of reasons, and are placed in remedial classes and programs such as alternate schools. During my time working in an alternate school, I was part of a small team of four staff, and we were trying to help the students navigate the school year and to survive difficult lives outside of school, which is still the problem for far too many. All First Nations people are trying to survive the world we are in, having been dealt a poor hand from a dominant society, and it's intense because our world is so small.*

John: In the mid-'80s, Joe was hired by the Vancouver School Board to be a childcare worker at the Outreach Alternate School in the First United Church at Hastings and Gore. The school is located at the centre of the downtown eastside in Vancouver, which is often described as the worst neighborhood in Canada. It is the hub of Vancouver's drug use, alcoholism, homelessness, prostitution, violence, crime, and many other social issues.

The year he spent there was a real education and a time of transition for him personally. He still had a couple of courses that he needed to do to finalize his degree from UVic, but he was almost done.

At the time Joe was working at the Alternate School, I rode the bus every day right past it, wearing a suit and tie on my way to my office on the sixth floor of the MacMillan Bloedel building on the corner of Georgia and Thurlow. Just like when I used to drive through the Tla'amin reserve, I saw the poverty, but I never stopped. The people I saw were typically passed out on the street, or drunk.

Many of them were members of First Nations. This is long before I understood anything about addiction or the history of inflicted trauma.

It was a small school. Two teachers and two childcare workers, including Joe, and about 20 kids. They were First Nations and from many different communities throughout BC. He knew some of their families from soccer and even had a cousin attending there. There were two people connected to the Tla'amin community. He had thought he had a tough upbringing, but it was a real eye-opener to see the challenges that some of the kids were facing. They were involved in the sex trade, gangs, and drugs. It was difficult to understand how they navigated going to school or even just getting through the day.

The other, longstanding, childcare worker was a strong First Nations woman from the North who now lives in the city and did a lot of work in the nonprofit sector, supporting the vulnerable population—women, mostly.

At 23, Joe wasn't much older than a lot of the students, who were 15 to 17. This allowed him to connect and relate to them and provide support on a different level than the other staff.

He was running physical education classes, taking them down to the Carnegie Centre Gymnasium, playing games and sports and supporting some of the work the teachers were doing. The other childcare worker would always have a plan of things they needed to sort through to just help the kids with life in general.

The education system had put these kids in alternate school because it was believed they wouldn't be successful in a mainstream school. The school system does not deal with First Nations kids well. If there is any kind of trouble, the system too often gives up on these children and prematurely assigns them to alternate programs. If the students weren't coming to classes, the staff knew they were hanging out in the streets somewhere. They were trying to help kids navigate their way through all the problems in their lives.

It was difficult to measure the success of their programs. The amount of time they had to have any substantial influence over the lives of these students was small relative to all the other influences in the teenagers' lives. Joe just tried to be someone they could talk to. Someone they could ask for help. That was the main part: giving them someone to trust. Joe did meet a few of them later; one had started playing soccer.

18. Victoria Friendship Centre

Joe: *For many reasons, such as lack of housing, jobs, or education available on Indian reserves, First Nations people often migrate to the urban centres. Living away from home can be challenging, without even the limited support the band office might offer if it was accessible. The inherent socio-economic challenges faced by First Nations people away from home can be intensified by the direct racism they experience trying to get along in a white-dominant society. Friendship Centres were established to provide a variety of valuable supports and services to First Nations and other Indigenous peoples who live in urban areas. They are essential gathering places for our peoples to come together, share in cultural and spiritual activities, and to be connected to Indigenous-led supports designed to help them navigate life in the city.*

John: Following a school year at the Alternate School in Vancouver, Joe was recruited by Alex Nelson, executive director at the Victoria Friendship Centre, to start running their programs. This is one of 25 Friendship Centres across British Columbia providing off-reserve support programs for First Nations people living in urban areas.

As director of programs, he supported summer recreation–related camps and drop-in programs for First Nations people to play sports and stay active. The Friendship Centre is a place where people belong. A place to go. A place that supports their many needs. There are other programs around employment and education, helping people complete Grade 12, addiction assistance, and counselling. It's a place to hold cultural events. The programs are offered at little or no cost, so anyone can attend.

Joe was seeing more of what city life was like for First Nations people. By then, more than half of all the BC First Nations population was living in urban settings. He experienced the challenges these people faced, but also the strength of their culture. This work also supported the expansion of his soccer environment; he became friends with others who played the game, in both mainstream leagues and First Nations tournaments. He met people from Nuu-chah-nulth, Kwakwaka'wakw, and Coast Salish from outside Tla'amin.

Dano Thorne from Cowichan, who had played soccer with Joe in England, worked for Joe at the Friendship Centre. While Joe served as director of programs, Dano was a program manager. Dano had always taken on leadership roles beyond soccer, developing skills as a life coach and suicide prevention mentor.

Joe was charged with organizing and supporting the annual First Peoples Festival, held on the BC Day long weekend at the Royal BC Museum in Victoria—another experience that helped ground him in what life was like for First Nations people generally. He got to know many new people and observe how their culture was integrated into their lives.

Through the centre, he got to know Alex Nelson well. The Kwakwaka'wakw man, from Kingcome, played at UVic back before Joe did, playing for Coach Brian Hughes. He knew a lot of the same players and had been in the same program as Joe at UVic. They first became acquainted as rivals playing soccer in Native ball. Joe's teams had played a lot of tough games against Alex's, but whenever Joe's team didn't enter a tournament, he'd be asked by Alex to play with his team.

Alex, along with his wife, Nella, who worked in the education system in Victoria, have a generous heart and soul. Their house has always been a meeting place, somewhere people could belong. To Joe, Alex was like a big brother, often inviting him over for dinner and sometimes to stay with them.

The couple also did a lot of work supporting Alex's people from Kwakwaka'wakw. Kids from Alert Bay and other relatives would live at their house in Victoria so they could go to school in the city because there wasn't opportunity at home. The value of family and extended family that Alex and Nella exemplified by looking after those kids was extraordinary. In taking care of them through their many difficulties, they also experienced a lot of heartache. Alex, in his generosity, always recognized that most people are doing their best to live their best life.

The kids hosted by Alex and Nella would often play soccer on one of the teams Alex put together just to help youth participate. Joe would play with those teams and sometimes helped out with the organizing. Alex also helped plan a celebration in Kingcome that included a soccer tournament.

A long time ago, Tla'amin teams used to travel up the coast by fish boat. Joe brought a young team from Tla'amin to play in the tournament so they could understand and honour those who came before them. They were able to learn hands-on about their rich soccer history. Fish boats were organized to get them there, so they had the full, inspired experience. Some of the older guys they spoke with reminisced about playing against Tla'amin teams, including some of Norman's uncles. They shared stories about what great players they were.

These kinds of activities help younger people understand their people and community. The Tla'amin youth taking part in this tournament witnessed more tradition being expressed in the communities farther up the coast than they did in their own community, which had been hit harder by assimilation.

Unfortunately, for every positive story there were many negative outcomes. I asked Joe if he struggled emotionally, dealing with the difficult issues, including teen suicide, he faced while working at the Alternative School and the Friendship Centre—watching people struggle so much in life.

Joe: *The First Nations people I met while at the Alternate School and at the Victoria Friendship Centre were like an extended family to me. Some were actually my blood relatives, and many were my brothers and sisters in our First Nations way. We are all one, and it was my job to do what I could to help them. To do the best I could for them.*

As First Nations people, we must take care of one another. It was an important role, and I was doing work with meaning and purpose. It also gave me a chance to meet many First Nations people from many places over the years, who were trying to survive in the same world I had been trying to navigate all my life.

Part 6

TREATY – BEING TLA'AMIN – RECOGNITION

19. What's in a Name?

John: Some people are campaigning today to change the name of Powell River. I hope that by the time this is published, it will have happened, but at the time of writing it feels like it will take some time. I have seen signs stating: "We love our town—Powell River." There is a lot to love about the town, but the name isn't one of them. Social media responses have pushed back on a name change, with comments including:

"What's next? Rewriting history?"

How about learning some history? Before settlers arrived in Tla'amin territory, Tla'amin people lived sophisticated, abundant, and rich lives, in balance with the land. The arrival of Europeans, their intentional spread of disease, theft of land, and disregard for sustainability robbed the Tla'amin people of their riches. Resources were sold or destroyed by settlers, with no compensation to First Nations.

"If history never happened, they wouldn't have the wonderful things they are blessed with today."

Powell River was a wonderful, rich town for white people to grow up in. The people of Tla'amin were not invited to participate, even though the resources that drove the settlers' prosperity came from their territory.

"The Powell River Company built homes, a hospital and schools."

Great, except these developments were not available to "Indians" at the time.

"Nothing will make them happy. You can't keep giving and giving for mistakes that happened."

What is it you think you keep giving? First Nations people are poorer, have higher rates of incarceration, live shorter lives, and have poorer health.

"The term 'the white man' is racist toward people of European descent, too."

This is classic white fragility.

These comments illustrate just how far we collectively must go to acknowledge our past and work towards reconciliation.

There is also an urgency for the change that I didn't initially understand. Support for a name change is gaining momentum and it seems only a matter of time and generational change, for the community to finally move forward with it. That unfortunately does nothing for the elders that will leave us before it happens.

Sadly, Les Adams passed away during the writing of this book. During one of the final conversations Joe had with him, Les wanted to talk about the name change of the community hospital from Powell River General to qathet General. This positive step was triggering for Les. Les, who to Joe was always a strong-minded leader who spent his life looking after his family, people at work, on the soccer field, and in the community as chief of the Sliammon Indian Band, was very emotional about the name change. This strong man who had no fear of a bear expressed deep sadness and emotion as he talked to Joe about pain he felt from a lifetime of racism experienced by himself, his family and the Tla'amin people. The name change to Les was an indication that for the first time the Tla'amin people have been seen by others with dignity and respect through the acknowledgment of the truth of the harms caused by the former namesake of Powell River. Les shared with Joe that his grandmother taught him the importance of always standing strong by your truths. The name change is an indication of the power of truth that is required as we further the journey towards reconciliation.

We are experiencing an increasing focus on recognizing that First Nations people need to be part of their own solution. Are we there yet? Mostly no. As we try to make progress, how do the two parties learn to trust one another, based on all the things that have been done to First Nations, and the fact that people don't trust them for other reasons?

A long prevailing attitude among too many non–First Nations people is that they're willing to help the First Nations community, as long as they don't become better off than *us*. But maintaining "less than" status doesn't work for either side. You can't be okay if First Nations people die sooner, or are less educated. Nor can they always be poorer. That is what needs to change. They deserve equity; to regain some of what is rightfully theirs.

The 2015 Truth and Reconciliation Commission (TRC) report defined reconciliation as "establishing and maintaining a mutually respectful relationship between Aboriginal and non-Aboriginal peoples in this country. For that to happen, there must be awareness of the past, acknowledgement of the harm that has been inflicted, atonement for the causes, and actions to change the behaviour."[28]

Truth and Reconciliation doesn't appear to be something our government has the will to move forward at the pace needed, so it is time we as individuals acknowledge that deliberate actions were taken by government to dehumanize First Nations people and that systemic racism exists. This is not something that is happening somewhere else. It is happening in your community, wherever you are in Canada. We can each make a personal commitment to anti-racism and support First Nations in reclaiming their identity and language. We can hold our leaders accountable.

My starting point in advocating for reconciliation and equitable treatment of First Nations starts with me recognizing my own truth. I am acknowledging my past blindness and acceptance of First Nations being treated as "less than." I am continuing to listen and learn. Unfortunately, too many of us continue to live in denial.

In October 2021, former prime minister Jean Chretien claimed he had not been made aware of residential school abuse while he served as Indian Affairs minister (1968-1974), despite significant evidence to the contrary. It amazes me that someone of his stature would rather look like he was completely ignorant about what his department was involved in than tell the truth. We seem to have a habit of electing

---

28   http://publications.gc.ca/collections/collection_2015/trc/IR4-7-2015-eng.pdf

people with bad memories. Rather than making such statements, he could have done so much more for First Nations and his own legacy by telling the truth. We can all do more by telling the truth. We can take actions, like changing offensive names, that take very little effort but would mean so much to First Nations people.

20. A Foot in Each World

Joe: *While at university, I started learning more about the things that had been done to my people, not because this history was covered in university classes but through things I heard and learned through conversations with First Nations people. Things that were never talked about at home. Being older and outside the day-to-day happenings of my community, I became more aware of the impact settler colonialism had had on them. I could see their situation wasn't solely the fault of our people. Things were the way they were for a reason. I knew enough to realize that, while I found it difficult to live within the colonial-induced dysfunction of my own community, I didn't fit or belong exclusively in the white world, either. I felt the urge to spend more time at home and be part of the community, as well as to begin to denounce the racism I had tried to ignore in the past.*

John: Joe often says today that he has a foot in each world, but at that point he didn't feel he had a foot firmly planted in either. When doing treaty or other consulting work, he was always aware of the need to protect himself. He would manage safe conversations with First Nations and non–First Nations people, understanding how contentious some of the issues he was working on were. Playing soccer, he would only talk about soccer, and keep it very soccer-focused. He would have a beer afterwards and enjoy the camaraderie without getting into some of the very complex issues he was immersed in off the field. Plus, at times he just wanted to be a soccer player.

As he spent more time at home, his thinking and understanding of the impact on his people progressed. He began asking: at what point would they take responsibility and stop doing harm to each other? They couldn't just be victims. They needed to be part of the solution. They needed to go "meet the ball."

Every day, Joe wakes up and reminds himself that he is no longer going to tolerate being "less than." Some days he feels good about it; on others he still feels he is being pushed down. He will keep doing it, but he does get tired of having to explain that he belongs.

First Nations people have differing connections to traditional teachings, culture, and values. Some have a complete link, others have had it totally stripped away, and there is every variation in between. Colonization left too many First Nations people trying to understand life with little or no identity.

Joe talks about how amazing it is to hear so many languages when walking around downtown Vancouver. The sad fact is he seldom hears First Nations languages. They had that taken away. Many don't carry enough of their history and traditions, because so much of that was also taken away. They were oppressed, and their oppressors acted like they were doing them a favour. They were told to stop eating deer, stop eating fish. *Here's some flour, get diabetes, and while we're at it, take one of these blankets.*[29]

Many First Nations languages have become endangered.[30] Tla'amin, K'omoks, Homalko and Klahoose are part of the language group called Éy7á7juuthem (EYE-a-jooth-um). As of 2018, out of a population of 2,037 people, there are only 47 fluent speakers left. There are 106 who somewhat understand it, and 361 who are in the learning process. There is an effort to protect the language, which contains much of their culture, but it is a race against time.

The First Nations people I have met on this project have all been generous to me in helping tell Joe's history. They have been patient in describing situations where most people would be outwardly furious. I have watched videos of Elsie Paul, Tla'amin Nation Knowledge Keeper, telling stories with humour and kindness. Sulksun, Coast Salish Knowledge Keeper, speaks with wit and generosity. Every First Nations person I have met on this project is humble, yet also proud, and maybe angry. I am sure there are exceptions, but those

---

29   Suggesting blankets may have been deliberately infected with smallpox. https://www.thecanadianencyclopedia.ca/en/article/smallpox#

30   https://maps.fpcc.ca 2018

exist in any community, even without the level of mistreatment that First Nations have had to endure.

Joe and I started this project at the onset of the Covid pandemic. When travel began to open up again, we made a trip to Vancouver Island for a few days of golf. While lined up for the ferry from Tsawwassen, we bumped into one of the First Nations guys Joe played soccer with and against. It was wonderful to see the instant connection and the enthusiasm for soccer the two men shared. The stories flowed easily. It was a great reminder to me of the fun and passion shared by First Nations people. We must get to know each other better, simply as people, while acknowledging the special role of First Nations.

21. Acknowledgment

Joe: *I, and other First Nations people, are not asking everyone to continually feel guilty or bad about what has happened in the past, as the truth comes to the surface. However, now that the truth is on the table, we do hold non-Indigenous settlers, who have all benefited from the unearned privilege generated by our history of settler colonialism, responsible for what happens moving forward. We want and deserve social and legal justice. Since settler colonialism was initiated, First Nations people have lived under a separate, imposed set of laws and policies meant to deny our rights and title and to remove us from our lands and cause us great harms. We are now at a time where Canada realizes it can no longer deny the rights of Indigenous peoples and that Indigenous-specific racism must end. Moving forward, things will continue to be different; the First Nations peoples' worldview is different from that of Western society, and self-determination will mean our governments will not be run the same as other Western communities. That's okay. What isn't okay is what has happened in the past.*

John: When I first started hearing the verbal acknowledgment of unceded or traditional First Nations lands at the start of meetings or events, I didn't like it. I didn't understand the need. Joe and I had a lot of back and forth as I tried to understand his perspective and began to feel comfortable with what I was acknowledging.

I now appreciate that I am respectfully acknowledging First Nations having been on the land long before European colonization, as well as their important traditional relationship with, and stewardship of, the land. I am acknowledging that First Nations lived abundant, rich lives in balance with the land. They lived using complex and effective trade and governance systems and were healthy, hardworking people until settler colonization forced them into isolation, poverty, starvation, and death while settlers made money off the resources. The harm continues today, as too many First Nations people die poor in a rich land. In making land acknowledgements, I am supporting the need for reconciliation of land title, access, and self-determination.

Reconciliation requires open negotiations that acknowledge First Nations title exists over unceded land in British Columbia.

Too often, this statement is met by a conversation-stopping response of, "Even though that may be true, it doesn't matter, because we are not going anywhere." We can't let that be the end of the discussion. We can't accept First Nations people living as "less than."

In the words of Arthur Manuel, in the book he co-authored with Grand Chief Ron Derrickson, *Unsettling Canada: A National Wake-Up Call,*"[31]

"We cannot continue to remain poor in our own territories while governments make all the decisions and corporations get rich off our land. We have to be recognized as decision-makers regarding our territories and to be remunerated fairly for access to our lands and resources. Any fair arrangement has to recognize our Aboriginal title ownership of our territories today and into the future, and we have to be paid for access to our land and resources."

While definitive about the need for recognizing title ownership, Manuel and Derrickson also acknowledge that the reconciliation process requires reasonable nation-to-nation talks. Canada needs to come to the table ready to take real action.

"[W]hen we speak about reclaiming a measure of control over our lands, we obviously do not mean throwing Canadians off it and sending them back to the countries they came from—that is the kind of *reductio ad absurdum* that some of those who refuse to acknowledge our title try to use against us. We know that for centuries Canadians have been here building their society, which, despite its failings, has

---

31   *Unsettling Canada: A National Wake-Up Call.* Arthur Manuel, Grand Chief Ronald M. Derrickson. Kindle Edition.

become the envy of many in the world. All Canadians have acquired a basic human right to be here. We also know that Canada does not have the astronomical amount of money it would cost to pay us for the centuries of use of our lands. We are certainly asking for compensation for the illegal seizures, but those amounts we can discuss."

We also need to recognize that less than 6 percent of land in British Columbia is considered by the federal and provincial governments to be privately owned. The remaining 94 percent has been allocated as Crown land. An appropriate level of title, decision-making, participation in the riches coming from the land, and access to land and resources must be agreed upon.

Non-—First Nations people often complain about perceived favouritism toward First Nations people, completely ignoring their loss of land and resources. The complainers don't account for the systemic racism that made it difficult for First Nations people to get meaningful jobs or a loan.

First Nations people have been denied the opportunity to amass generational wealth. Take the example of home ownership in Powell River. A family who purchased a waterfront home for $40,000 in town 50 years ago will find that home's value has increased by 2,000 percent. This gain was not available to the people of Tla'amin. Then there is lost income due to intentional acts, such as the cost of fishing licenses increasing to the point that First Nations people could not afford them. These are just examples. They don't come anywhere near telling the entire story.

I have come to understand the theft of First Nations' resources, the recovery process, and the impact of the conditions the BC First Nations people were forced to live in. I have become far more sensitive to the issues they are addressing. It's not just about righting a wrong with fair compensation. It's about equity.

Not having had control of their lives for over 150 years has perpetuated the problem. The government never intended the Indian Act to help them be a successful part of society. Its intent was to force them to assimilate as the door mat of society. The whole notion of identity is critically important, but this government control has broken down much of who they are. First Nations people must find a way through a lot of ugly things that weren't their doing.

For equity to happen, we must work to see things from the First Nations perspective as well as our own. The white settler colonial system is bent in favour of the majority, which has more experience in negotiation and managing its way through it. While the divide between us is not as great as it was 150, 100 or even 50 years ago, it still exists. First Nations deserve to have their perspective heard, in line with their rights.

We continue to undercompensate First Nations for harms done. They are survivors of a government that ensured they were far less prosperous than the rest of us. Think of how the term *reconciliation* is used in financial settings: it's about balancing accounts. When you reconcile accounts, you don't just adjust one side of the equation; you adjust both to find a balance. We need to adjust privilege as well as oppression by working collaboratively. We can't continue to focus only on oppression.

Consider another historic example of a relationship between the privileged and the oppressed. The women's suffrage movement pushed for the right for women to vote. The women in this case were the oppressed, and while they could protest, they needed the support of the privileged class—men, in this case—to recognize their rights. They didn't need men to tell them what they wanted or needed. They were the best judge of that. They just needed men to assure their equality. In the same way, white people, as the privileged class, need to be the ones to assure First Nations' equality, but First Nations need to determine what equality looks like for them. (Unfortunately, the women's rights issue also illustrates how real change takes time.) Of course, when white women were finally given the opportunity to vote, First Nations women did not get the same right.

Joe*: The Truth and Reconciliation Commission report Call to Action #43 states that the United Nations Declaration on the Rights* *of Indigenous Peoples should be adopted and implemented as the framework for reconciliation. This ensures that reconciliation must be "on our terms," which brings forward the challenge of discourse among ourselves as First Nations people. There are many differing points of view among the 203 First Nations in BC because of who they are, where they are from, and how they relate to their hereditary systems and teachings and values. The impact of settler colonialism on First Nations has resulted in these differing points of view. There are a lot of voices to be heard and nation rebuilding to be done as an integral part of the reconciliation process.*

John: There are good people doing good things to move forward, with a shifting of the tide towards reconciliation. We see efforts being made to teach First Nations languages, and First Nations names for places are being shared on road signs and walkways. We also continue to see many setbacks, with racism observed in colonial institutions like banks, museums, and hospitals, but that can't stop us from moving forward.

When we speak of reconciling and acknowledging the "less than" treatment of First Nations, it can feel as though we are in a never-ending cycle of discussing the negative things. For First Nations, losing the "less than" perception starts with having their rights recognized and reconciled. It means re-establishing their connection to their territory, to determine their future and the future of coming generations in a modern context. Difficult conversations are required, to acknowledge the wrongs that have been imposed on First Nations, for us to start the work of making things right. These negatives should not be a means of labeling First Nations people; they are simply facts that need to be acknowledged.

22. Back to Tla'amin

1989–1994

Joe: *As a child, I didn't understand what the reserve system was all about. We all just lived together in the community outside of town and struggled with life on a daily basis. I didn't understand that all the nice houses on the waterfront in Powell River were built on our traditional lands, yet I wasn't welcome there. I didn't know the mill was built on our original village site, at the mouth of a salmon-bearing river. I didn't know that river was dammed to generate power for the mill, which generated great wealth for the people of Powell River and only a very small number of our people would work there. The salmon were gone, and the river turned into a lake. I had friends in school with cabins on that lake and I thought, wow, they were lucky. They were haves and the people of Tla'amin were clearly the have-nots. Now I recognize that all of that is in the heart of Tla'amin territory, a rich territory which my people had occupied for thousands of years, but now, thanks to settler colonialism, it somehow belongs to someone else and we have no say in the matter.*

John: Joe left the Friendship Centre after three years, when he was recruited by the BC Ministry of Aboriginal Affairs to work in the division of First Citizens Fund and Economic Development. This was the first of a few government roles Joe held where he lasted only a year. His ambition for change was more urgent than a government role would accommodate.

A year later, Joe moved on when Robert Harry, the chief in Tla'amin at the time, reached out and encouraged him to come home and do some work in economic development. Robert had been Joe's baseball coach when he was a teenager. At that point, Joe was ready to go home. Starting with his co-op terms, he had always felt a responsibility to return at some point and work for his own people, to make things better. As a community, they needed people who had gone away to get a postsecondary education to come back home.

After a year at home, he received an offer from the Ministry of Aboriginal Affairs to take the role of director of the department he had formerly worked in. It was a great opportunity for development, so with agreement from the band administration, he went back to Victoria to become director. A year later, he again felt the need to get back home.

Approaching his thirties, he had dedicated himself to making things better for his people. Having pushed aside his childhood fears as he accumulated experiences inside and outside the community, he had a much clearer perception of what had happened to his people. They weren't the way they were because they wanted to be that way.

Band administrator Joe Mitchell started taking Joe with him to events such as the Coast Salish All Chiefs meetings, which gave him an education on the 54 Coast Salish bands, their history and connection to the land, and "Indian politics." An amazing storyteller, Joe Mitchell exposed Joe to much more of the traditional teachings and to many different chiefs' gatherings. With his mentorship, Joe learned by watching and doing, as had been their people's practice for generations. What he received from Joe Mitchell had a great influence on him personally, and in all the work he has done in support of First Nations in BC.

Having been supported with his education, he felt a responsibility to give back to his community. He had been honoured by Robert Harry's move to bring him back, and he felt confident and ready to have a greater positive impact on Tla'amin. But it turned out that his view of the world and appetite to get things done was somewhat out of sync with the community, which had taken to hiring consultants, mostly white, whose value wasn't all that clear to him. Yet it was apparent that the community did need and want help. Joe recognized that, with his education and experience of colonial ways as well as his knowledge of the people, he could be a positive alternative to employing non–First Nations consultants who didn't fully understand the people they were tasked to help.

Joe proposed doing the work as a consultant. He would work for the community half-time—a proposal that worked for them in part because he was already driving them crazy. The other half of his time, he would go work for other communities. He also anticipated being able to bring some good ideas back home.

Joe recognized the need to bring the best people possible to the table. He was pleased to start working with Roy Francis, who had gone to school about the same time and had graduated from Simon Fraser University.

Both worked half-time for Tla'amin, devoting the other half of their time to a joint consulting business, exploring issues of employment, training, economic development, land management, small business development, etc. They went about the process of finding work, partnering, and building their reputation, and grew their consultancy quickly. Being an entrepreneur was fun for Joe and the very opposite of working under the Indian Act. The partners had freedom of choice to work with their people wherever they chose. They were not confined to work on initiatives on their own reserve only, or on any specific reserve. They worked across the province and had the opportunity to participate in various initiatives that generated new and innovative ideas to bring back home. They didn't have to work for a band or be employed by a band to do work for their people.

When the treaty work came in, however, it ended up being all-consuming for both of them.

23. Fighting for What Was Already Theirs

Joe: *There was little thought of war at the time of first contact, although some First Nations people now say maybe there should have been. Our people chose to help care for Europeans when they first landed on our shore after their long trips at sea. They didn't arrive strong. First Nations people showed the European people how to survive and live on these lands. Our people had the intention of learning more from these new arrivals. An opportunity to live a life guided by the best of both worlds. Sharing and stewarding the lands for future generations. Living side by side, in a spirit of mutual respect and dignity.*

John: First Nations were willing to share the land with the Europeans and were told by the British specifically that they wanted that as well. First Nations had been sharing the land for years.

It turns out, their versions of sharing were quite different. The First Nations' view of the natural hierarchy starts with the land, then the plants and trees, then the animals, and finally the people, which meant they had no concept of land ownership. Land was something they needed to respect and sustain. The actions of the new arrivals, on the other hand, said, "Well, no, we don't really share. We have fee simple ownership, and it's either mine or it's yours. And by the way, most of it's going to be mine, even though you are on it all now."

I grew up on land that was unceded.

In those early discussions, First Nations people had no idea the forests would be clear-cut and the fishery would disappear. For First Nations, it was about balancing relationships. They also trusted when they were told they could retain access to their land. The result is that Aboriginal peoples in Canada comprise 4.9 percent of the population yet own only 0.2 percent of the land that they previously occupied.[32] There isn't much doubt in that circumstance which group will be poor and which group will be rich.

Arrangements were made that were not honoured by Canada. And it's not as if this behaviour was a one-time occurrence. It continues to be difficult for First Nations to trust the federal government.

1763 – Royal Proclamation Signed by King George III

King George III, in 1763, signed a proclamation that confirmed under colonial law that Aboriginal title exists until a treaty is signed. It directed any settler on unceded land to leave that land.

The proclamation is written in the English legal language of its day, so it can be tricky to read, as the following excerpt shows, but First Nations peoples clearly had inherent rights to the land, and no Europeans were permitted to live on their lands without a treaty being signed.

"… all persons whatever who have either willfully or inadvertently seated themselves upon any Lands within the Countries above described, or upon any other Lands which, not having been ceded to or purchased by Us, are still reserved to the said Indians as aforesaid, forthwith to remove themselves from such Settlements."[33]

The Royal Proclamation is the starting point of written evidence under colonial law of pre-existing rights and title of First Nations. Title wasn't *granted* to First Nations. They had always had it, and therefore had a right to it. Sadly, settlers in BC chose to ignore First Nations rights, and the Indian Act precluded First Nations from arguing in court on this subject until 1951.

---

32   *Unsettling Canada: A National Wake Up Call.* Arthur Manuel, Grand Chief Ronald M. Derrickson. Kindle Edition.
33   https://Indigenousfoundations.arts.ubc.ca/royal_proclamation_1763/

Shifting legal landscape

Joe: *We are taught to recognize and honour the leaders who came before us who dedicated themselves to fight for our rights, as activists or in the courts. Once First Nations could legally hire lawyers, case law was advanced, thanks to the courage and commitment of First Nations leaders to fight for their rights. This was a difficult undertaking, as the government's opening position in court was that we didn't exist. In contrast to the Royal Proclamation of 1763, where the British Crown recognized our title, government lawyers stated that our history was illegitimate, and our oral history didn't matter. Many great First Nations Leaders have dedicated their lives to fight for the recognition of our rights and title, and it continues today.*

(Take note of the number of years some of these cases took to get through the Supreme Court.[34])

1973 –Supreme Court rules that the Nisga'a had title before the settlers arrived

Frank Calder[35] and several Elders sued the Province of British Columbia in 1967, stating that their rights, based on occupation of their land, had never been extinguished. The decision on the land claim case was split on the issue of whether the Nisga'a had valid title, but importantly the court did acknowledge for the first time that aboriginal title to land existed prior to colonization.

---

34   https://www.lib.sfu.ca/help/research-assistance/subject/criminology/
      legal-information/Indigenous-scc-cases
35   Frank Calder was a groundbreaker, just as this case was. He was the first Status
      Indian to attend the University of British Columbia and was elected as the first
      Indigenous member of the BC Legislature in 1949, the first year Indigenous
      peoples were allowed to vote in BC elections. His first speech in the legislature
      called for a bill of rights. He was always fighting for Indigenous rights.

1982 – Canadian Constitution Act

The Canadian Constitution Act was passed in 1982. Section 35 of the Act[36] affirmed existing Aboriginal and treaty rights. The Constitution did not *grant* rights; it recognized rights that already existed.

Early drafts of the Constitution excluded any reference to First Nations rights. First Nations reacted with aggressive and determined activism, highlighted by the Constitutional Express, led by George Manuel, then president of the Union of BC Indian Chiefs. He rented two trains to carry concerned First Nations protestors from Vancouver to Ottawa. The media attention got people listening, and public support started to build. First Nations delegations also made their way to the United Nations and the United Kingdom Parliament to gain international support. The Constitutional Express is seen today as one of the most informative and effective protests in Canadian history.

Under this pressure from First Nations leaders, who had gone to extraordinary lengths with limited resources and in the face of settler colonial racism, the Canadian Constitution was finally modified to specify that Aboriginal rights and the right to self-determination exist.

The 1984 Guerin decision is named for Delbert Guerin, chief of the Musqueam Indian Band at the time. The federal government, in 1958, on behalf of the Musqueam Indian Band, leased land to the Shaughnessey Golf Course. In the process, they misled the Musqueam Band on the terms of the deal the government had made with the golf club. In 1970, when the Musqueam learned the actual details of that deal, they brought the case to court and fought it through to the Supreme Court of Canada, eventually winning a $10 million settlement. The federal government was found to have breached its fiduciary responsibility. This set the precedent of the federal government having to act in the best interest of First Nations people in a trust-like relationship.

The 1990 Sparrow decision was the first challenge involving First Nations rights in the Supreme Court of Canada based on Section

---

36   https://Indigenousfoundations.arts.ubc.ca/constitution_act_1982_section_35/

35 of the Constitution Act. This section acknowledged the existence of Aboriginal rights and established criteria for determining what constitutes government infringement of Aboriginal rights as contained in the Constitution. The original charge in 1984, against Ronald Sparrow of Musqueam for fishing with an illegal net, was overturned by the Supreme Court, which determined that fishing in his traditional territory was within his rights. The Supreme Court ruling did not conclude that Aboriginal rights could never be infringed upon, only that if the federal government were to infringe on them, this action needed to be demonstrably justified.

The 1997 Delgamuukw decision. Gitxsan and Wet'suwet'en hereditary chiefs made a title claim in 1984 involving 58,000 square kilometers of their traditional territory in northern BC. They based their argument on never having ceded the land. The government of BC countered the claim, saying the province had full ownership. The Supreme Court eventually ruled that Aboriginal title rights to the land and its resources existed and that the government had the duty to consult and, in some cases, compensate for infringements of Aboriginal rights. It also established the importance and legitimacy of oral history.

The 2004 Haida Nation and the **2004 Taku River Tlingit decisions in the Supreme Court of Canada.**[37] Both cases, first brought to court in the early 1990s, further clarified that governments must consult with aboriginal communities. The Haida case involved tree farm licenses, and the Taku case involved road access to a mining site. The court agreed that the duty to consult doesn't require a formal title to be in place. The duty to consult arises when the government knows of Aboriginal title, ought to know of it, or there is a potential for right and title to exist.

The 2014 Tsilhqot'in decision in Supreme Court of Canada held that, for the purposes of rights and title, rights were established by showing regular and exclusive use of the land, and therefore, in 1983, when BC granted a commercial logging license on the

---

37   https://www.lawsonlundell.com/media/news/236_Negotiatorarticle.pdf

territory in question, it was in breach of its duty to consult with the First Nations. This was another unique test, as those occupying the territory were nomadic.

Each of these cases, along with many others, built on one another to set the direction for treaty discussions.

First Nations were gaining momentum, and corporations were growing concerned. They wanted access to timber and other resources, but their legal rights to the land and resources were being contested, with some success. These BC court cases were creating economic instability and putting pressure on government and industry in Canada to act.

24. Tla'amin Treaty Work

Joe: *It was a great honour to be asked to support the work of the Tla'amin Treaty negotiations. This was the most important work to do, as it was charting a path to officially become part of Canada and a blueprint for the future of the Tla'amin Nation that would be based on Tla'amin laws and values. It was also a tremendous opportunity to work closely with my community, unpack the issues we faced under the Indian Act, and to further understand our true Tla'amin identity and relationship to our territory. This was the most positive aspect of my role in the treaty process. Our connection to land and resources, and our long, desperate fight for survival drove home how important the treaty process really was.*

At the Treaty Table with Nancy Morgan, Legal Counsel

John: The Canadian and BC governments recognized the need to establish a process to work with First Nations to facilitate treaties.

They needed to reduce some of the province's business uncertainty due to land title claims.

In 1994, the Sliammon Indian Band (Tla'amin Nation) submitted a Statement of Intent to the British Columbia Treaty Commission to signal its interest in beginning negotiations on a modern-day treaty with the Government of Canada and the Province of BC.

Already working with the band on numerous initiatives, Joe had the honour of being asked by Chief Eugene Louie to lead the treaty work. To continue the work done earlier by so many First Nations people, they saw it as critical to begin by implementing a community-based structure. The Tla'amin Treaty Society for the Tla'amin People was created as a group to oversee the treaty process, rather than working through the band office, which operated under the Indian Act and had its own purpose.

With the support of the chief and council, a working team was developed with six equal participants, to balance their various perspectives. They didn't kick off with the idea of one lead negotiator, and they rejected the idea of using a non–First Nations chief negotiator, as had been done in some other communities. They also avoided having a single person as the face of the negotiations.

The participants would include two Technical Leaders, two Traditional Advisors, and two Political Leaders. Roy and Joe were appointed as the Technical Leaders. The Political Leaders changed following elections.

The purpose of Traditional Advisors was to ensure, through their knowledge, that Tla'amin history would be part of any discussion. Joe Mitchell and Norman were identified as the two Traditional Advisors for the negotiation team. Joe was certainly surprised by his dad putting up his hand for this role. He knew he had the language, but he had no idea he had the level of richness in him that he was about to bring to the process.

Joe Mitchell (left) and Norman Gallagher during their time as Traditional Advisors to the Tla'amin Treaty Process.

Through this work, Norman often became the teacher Joe had never had, working with the team and other members of the community to build the knowledge base that would confirm the negotiation mandate, protect the territory, and contribute to the continued effort to re-establish the identity of the Tla'amin people and their relationship to their lands.

To Joe, it was as if Norman had flipped the script. Up to this point, his dad, despite his knowledge of the language and of the past, had focused hard on modelling the behaviour he thought was needed to find success in the white world. Now he was talking with community members and explaining middens, fish traps, and canoe skids. He was suddenly a willing contributor.

In Joe's role as Technical Advisor, he was initially nervous speaking to Tla'amin Elders, feeling insecure about the gaps in his knowledge of his culture, language, and history. Their response was both positive and supportive. It was important for Joe to demonstrate his humility and willingness to incorporate Tla'amin knowledge into the negotiation process. They were also pleased to have their own people doing the work for the nation. The Treaty Society wanted to capture as much of their actual history as possible.

As chiefs and councils came and went in Tla'amin band elections, Joe played a more and more prominent role and was a constant in the process. Eventually he was given the title of Chief Negotiator. Through this lead role, he made clear it wasn't his intention to sell the process to anyone. It was the community that had to decide who they were.

With BC Premier Ujjal Dosanjh and Roy Francis during treaty discussion days.

They philosophically debated whether they were rediscovering and/or redefining their culture and teachings. While relying on the teachings of the past, they also needed to move forward and incorporate Western tools. After years on a path toward cultural genocide, to reverse course they had to rediscover their teachings and their values.

Joe had access to many prominent people, as Tla'amin was a lead table in the negotiations—meaning they were further along in the process than most in the province. They were capable, able to organize and get things done. Joe was on a steep learning curve.

The BC treaty process was launched through a collaboration of many BC First Nations, which became the First Nations Summit. It was important to learn from the experience of others such as the Nisga'a, who had a strong knowledge of title issues, having won their case for Aboriginal title. Joe was around the political leaders who were trying to establish by what means First Nations would have self-determination in Canada, and some who had established certain new benchmarks in case law related to the Nisga'a and Delgamuukw cases.

As a First Nations person, he was happy to push back against the Indian Act on behalf of his people. The treaty work offered a transformational opportunity to go further and negotiate their way out of the Act, but he was also aware it had to be done in a way that was good for his people and not another agreement, signed under duress, that would only address immediate issues, like housing and safe water.

Through the treaty process, Joe gained a greater understanding of rights and title and the importance of discipline during the negotiations. He also began to understand why some leaders, like Arthur Manuel, were against the treaty process and instead were pushing for sovereignty.

"The Canadian government has time and again proven itself lawless when it comes to Indigenous peoples. Despite losing more than 150 legal cases on Indigenous rights over the past fifteen years,

it insists that it is in control of the Indian agenda and that Indigenous peoples have no rights."[38]

Joe saw an opportunity with the process but always kept in mind that having no deal would be better than accepting a bad deal. Joe had heard the late Hereditary Chief Joe Mathias, of S̲k̲w̲x̲wú7mesh Úxwumixw – Squamish First Nation, say this, and he hung on to it. They needed to ensure they were generating wealth for multiple generations, and not fall into the trap of making a deal focused on short-term needs.

Joe worked with other leaders and other chief negotiators across the province on rights and title issues. He was attempting to create a collaborative agenda, knowing that one nation like Tla'amin was going to find it difficult to get concessions on its own. They didn't gain as much traction as he would have liked on this at the treaty table.

The treaty process, unfortunately, proved very divisive, the result of a culture of mistrust carried forward from the Indian Act. Joe wasn't immune from suspicion. He was seen as a have rather than a have-not. When he and others landed in Tla'amin in a helicopter following a tour of the proposed treaty area, rumours spread throughout the community that Joe had been given a helicopter. They wanted to know whether their family would get their fair share. The treaty made no sense to them, because it didn't deal with their most immediate needs. Joe lost many relationships during the treaty process due to this divide, and he recognized that this was largely the result of the lack of wellness in the community.

During the initial vote on the Agreement in Principle, Joe sat and listened quietly and intently to the votes being counted. He kept hearing "No. No. No. No." Working through the process in his mind, he wondered why so many didn't agree with what they themselves had put forward. It was hard to listen to the count, but he needed to

---

38   *Unsettling Canada: A National Wake-Up Call.* Arthur Manuel, Grand Chief Ronald
       M. Derrickson. Kindle Edition.

hear it. He describes this day as one of the most important moments in his career.

The vote was 51 percent against, 49 percent for. The division in the community had come through loud and clear; work had to be done to bring the people together.

Even if the vote had gone 51-49 in favour, it would not have been good enough for Joe. He was looking for a collaborative environment, rather than a divisive one. It would never work without more buy-in. Instead of people working together, there were people celebrating a narrow loss.

There were tough discussions during and following the process, because he was there with people he had grown up with. People his age or people who were older; people who had babysat him, or whom he looked up to. Their whole lives had been spent struggling with bad housing, poverty, and lacking wellness. Then they got into a treaty discussion, and suddenly everything changed. Now he was having difficult conversations with these people that he cared about. Joe understood the importance of governance and how to move it ahead, or the kinds of things that needed to be done to advance the community, and yet those folks he had known for so long didn't see it as an opportunity to move ahead.

A different approach was needed. Their treaty team tactics changed to a focus on enhancing consensus-building. It was no longer just Joe up there by himself trying to convince people. They initiated a process to engage families and have families choose who they wanted to speak for them: their trusted sources; knowledgeable people who were doing the work in the process.

Consistent with traditional methods, they brought in heads of families, and their spokesperson represented them with other heads of families to build consensus on how to move forward. When the vote came again two years later, it was 70 percent in favour of an Agreement in Principle (AIP) to continue with the process toward a final agreement. From that point, there was a need to build on that momentum, bringing people together.

Getting that collaborative support was important, and shortly after that vote, Joe felt it was time for him to move on from the Chief Negotiator role. The community needed to take the focus away from "Joe's" treaty, and all the good and bad that came with that, because there was still a lot of division. He did not want to get in the way of community members taking the time to understand for themselves what the deal was. It would be difficult to build more consensus if you were becoming a polarizing figure in the situation.

Joe intended to stay on in some capacity through the transition, but they chose to go on without him. It worked out well for him, as he was finally able to put his focus into health and wellness, and he was ready to get away from the pressure and the strain of it all.

As it turns out, if he had remained in the treaty role, and under the stress and division it involved, he might not have gone out and obtained the rapid treatment that allowed him to beat cancer. Changing jobs probably saved his life.

He did leave with concerns. Self-government requires a system that brings people together, and there was still a lot of work to be done.

This would be a long journey. Following the signing of the Agreement in Principle, Joe continued to articulate that no deal would be better than a bad deal. There were items they could work on and gain experience with before making the final decision. There was enough opportunity at that time to start trying to run businesses and to develop their own constitution. As they worked through their treaty process, it had to support their traditions and teachings, but it also had to make financial sense.

The people needed to be supported in improving their personal health and wellness. Having spent their lives in an Indian band now recognized as a First Nation, they needed to somehow develop leadership capable of seeing a world of possibilities beyond their current experience.

Unfortunately, as they moved forward from the AIP, support for the treaty negotiated with the government ended up narrowing again: a 52/48 split, but in favour. This was not a good situation, as the community remained divided and the consensus built during the AIP phase was lost. The team moved ahead regardless and signed a treaty, amid much opposition.

In the end, the treaty provided 8,223 hectares of fee-simple land, including 1,917 hectares of former reserve land. The settlement established title for Tla'amin of 2.6 percent of their traditional lands and included nothing from Lot 450.

25. Father, Son, and Grandson

Joe: *It's ironic that my dad became one of the Traditional Advisors, giving information they could draw their conclusions from in the treaty process. All those years of pushing me into the "white" world, and now he was sharing his knowledge about our past and who we are as Tla'amin people. I was so excited for the possibilities of what he could teach his grandchildren in the future.*

John: One very positive experience for Joe was providing his son with an opportunity to get to know his grandfather. They spent some time together and were beginning to build a strong bond. This was great for Joe to see, and he was hopeful for the years ahead, where the teacher of traditional knowledge that his father was becoming would directly benefit his son and his other grandchildren. In the visits Joe's son had with his grandfather during holidays and vacations, they would enjoy their time together and talk about sports. Norman showed a gentleness to his grandchildren that Joe had not seen before. He was able to become his best self and enjoyed being part of the community in ways he never had as a younger man. Unfortunately, his remaining years were limited.

Norman and Joe during treaty process. It's difficult to read Joe's thoughts as his dad is explaining something to him.

As father and son, through the treaty work, they maintained clear boundaries shaped by many turbulent years. Joe tried to treat him respectfully and professionally, as he would with anyone in the Traditional Advisor role. They had little interaction beyond that, as Joe was deep into carrying out the responsibilities he had as Chief Negotiator, and there was so much to be done by everyone. They were working with the community, third-party interests, other treaty tables, and of course the provincial and federal governments, which always seemed to have endless resources behind them.

To achieve the Agreement in Principle for the Sliammon First Nation in 2003 was a major step. Only a couple of other treaty tables in the province were able to achieve that milestone by that year. It was a landmark accomplishment for the community, and Norman was proud to be part of the work. It also marked the only time Joe remembers his dad saying he was proud of him. It was the first time he acknowledged Joe's leadership capabilities and recognized him as his own man.

Joe was happy for Norman; happy that the work he had been responsible to implement had so much value and meaning for his dad through the very knowledge and teachings he possessed, and the fact that the colonial experience was no longer going to dictate who he was. He became active and outgoing in a way Joe had never seen before. He was enjoying himself, and others were enjoying being with him.

Part 7

HEALTH AND WELLNESS

26. You Can't Always Work from a Deficit

Joe: *Health and wellness is such an important concept, one to keep top of mind every day. We have many First Nations teachings that contribute to achieving and living our best lives—to achieve the right balance of health and wellness. Specifically,* health *refers to being free from sickness or injury, whereas* wellness *means being in a state of good health. Settler colonialism purposefully inflicted poor health or caused sickness or injury and death to First Nations peoples, and has had no or little interest in the wellness of First Nations people. As a result, our narrative has gone from traditionally living a life of wellness within our rich territories to a discussion about how sick the First Nations population is and how our health outcomes are so poor compared to the settler population, who have benefited from unearned privilege at our expense through colonialism.*

Moving forward, I choose to focus on a health and wellness ideology that promotes our wellness from a strength-based perspective, front and centre, as we address the many healing journeys that are required to move beyond the negative impacts of settler colonialism. Today there are many great First Nations strength-based considerations that have sustained us for thousands of years and that we can rely on to ensure our children and future generations can strive for a life focused on the positive.

Supporting Suicide Awareness Relay

Additional FNHA wellness activity

Joe learned as he got older what it means to be Coast Salish from the Tla'amin community. This knowledge had been missing for him, growing up, so his wellness was initially dependent on soccer. He was at his best when he was playing. If he went off the rails, soccer was always what brought him back to where he needed to be. Initially it was an escape, but at the end of the day, it represented a form of strength-based wellness. It was something like, "Yeah, go get out of all this shit and go for a run." *Go play. Go have fun. Go be with good people with like minds and challenge yourself to be the best you can be.* Ultimately that attitude is a significant part of wellness.

Joe has always lived in Coast Salish territory. He has traveled to many other places, but he always feels at home, connected, when he is in his territory. When he does travel, it feels good to get home. Wellness for Joe is about gaining a greater understanding of what he's been taught, and how those learnings and values are consistent with First Nations philosophy.

When he did the treaty work, he began to understand traditional place names and how they related to people and their identities and responsibilities. The way Coast Salish use language to play sports; the teachings; the ceremonies; the spirit baths. Understanding and embracing all of that became part of his sense of wellness. Those are things he hangs on to, so that as he walks around in the world with brown skin, he knows who he is.

Joe didn't have the benefit of Elders teaching him in his youth, but he still had a feeling of being at home in the community; a sense of the deeper meaning. He has gained a lot from working in the health field and connecting with Knowledge Keepers around issues focused on First Nations healing. When he goes to a sweat, he recognizes that he is often older than those carrying the knowledge. First Nations societies are seeing a lot of roles coming back and being taught to younger generations. He's pleased to see young people engaged in culture and teachings.

Joe emphasizes the need to create supportive structures in these communities. It's important to talk about healing, but there is also a need to focus on wellness. People can't always operate from a deficit. They need to go forward with strength and self-determination to address symptoms such as drug and alcohol abuse that affect too many First Nations people. They need to move forward with a positive, wellness-based, strength-based mindset.

It's important to approach these critical issues by taking into consideration various points of view, particularly those of young people and Elders. The impact of yesterday's traumas is different today, but it remains prevalent. People need to find new ways to navigate their future and learn from the past. They need an environment where people can live their best lives.

Joe understands that it will take time to develop the capacity to look back, understand what happened, and put it in the right context. Eventually, history can stop being an anchor weight. Instead, it can become part of your identity and understanding of your story, and you can free yourself. There are many traditional teachings around this kind of medicine and freeing yourself of burdens.

Joe has an appetite for seeing community pride built around culture and ceremony, but this vision is not fully developed in him. It's just that he wasn't raised that way. Many young people are doing the work of reconnecting with culture, and particularly the gift of learning their language.

Full expression of cultural teachings and traditions is tied to the land and the resources it provides. For First Nations, culture is an expression of their relationship with the land: the food they eat, the materials used, the language they use. It's all connected to the land. Family names are connected to places.

The stories they tell and dances they perform have spiritual meaning. Just like the Christian stories of creation, First Nations have creation stories, which are their truth. The Squamish have stories about the two twins [39] (also known in Vancouver as the Lions) and their meaning; these stories are about two sisters who brought warring factions together to create lasting peace. The challenge is to

---

39   https://www.legendsofvancouver.net/two-sisters-vancouver-bc

keep such stories alive and the connections strong. For a long period, potlatches and other expressions of First Nations culture and traditions were deemed illegal by the government and evil by the church. This is why acknowledging territory is so important.

27. kʼʷunəmɛn

Joe: *The giving of names in Tla'amin was disrupted by the church and other forms of settler colonialism, but there has been a resurgence. Knowing how to do this naming properly is important, but that has been a challenge for Tla'amin, as it's a forgotten part of our history. We have had to rediscover and redefine our ways by leveraging the teachings from our Elders and sometimes neighbouring Coast Salish communities so that they work in our environment. Sometimes this can result in disagreement, but the nation has been able to re-establish the important and fundamental practice of giving names. Receiving a Tla'amin name is a great honour, and I am forever grateful to the matriarch Elders who made the decision to bestow this honour upon me almost 20 years ago. However, most people will continue to know me by the colonial name that my mom and dad gave me at birth. I go by that name to honour them, as I recognize they did the best they could for me at a time where the systems around us were denying who we were as Tla'amin people. I do go by my Tla'amin name as a secondary name, to reaffirm who I am and where I am from in this evolving environment. It is now my responsibility to find a way to have the same honour bestowed on my son, someday in the future.*

John: Indian agents were charged with recording names of "Indians" on reserves, and rather than trying to understand First Nations names, they simply gave them Christian names. Their focus was on assimilation.

In the case of Joe's great-great-grandparents, it is likely Mary was given a Tla'amin name but then identified as Mary. Mary's husband Joe's name is less clear. Coming from Chile and of Spanish descent, he may have been called Jose. This seems to be lost history.

When Joe was home working on the treaty process, a group of Elders held a naming ceremony for four people, including Joe. It was a tremendous honour for him to be recognized by the Elders and to be given a name representing how they saw him. You don't select your own name; the Elders do it for you. Through this ceremony, Joe was given a stronger attachment to Tla'amin. In his case, kʷunəmɛn: "one with vision." A very appropriate name.

His name recognizes him as a spokesperson and a leader in the community. This name reinforced the idea that no matter where he goes, no matter where he lives, he is part of Tla'amin. This is an important teaching that connects him with home.

Traditionally First Nations members were given names that someone else had carried before them, for reasons connected to history or responsibilities or where they were from. Names would carry on in families. Some people know the names that were used in their families. In Joe's case, they didn't, so the name they gave him was a description of who he is.

Tla'amin people have lost much of their language, oral history, and their connection to the land, territory, and their culture. Bringing back traditions like the giving of names is significant.

Shortly after Joe's son was born, he brought him home to meet his family and others in the community. During a naming ceremony, he was given the Tla'amin nickname of Qwoke Ness, which means baby killer whale. At some point, he will receive his full name.

Joe had found his identity through soccer, through experiences in his community including the treaty process, through a broader experience with First Nations in an urban setting. Now he had a greater sense of belonging, as kʷunəmɛn.

28. Sad Introduction to the Healthcare System

Joe: *Health and wellness are not new to First Nations. Historically we lived a life primarily free from illness and injury and enjoyed a state of wellness supported by our medicines and healers and a productive lifestyle within our rich territories. Unfortunately, this has been disrupted dramatically by settler colonialism for just over the past 150 years.*

As Joe was leaving the Tla'amin treaty process in 2005, he came across a posting for a job working in health for the First Nations Summit. The Summit, initially set up to support First Nations communities with ongoing treaty negotiations, had expanded into other areas where socio-economic gaps existed for First Nations.

It piqued his interest, having become so aware of the roadblocks, dysfunction and dependency that existed in First Nations communities resulting from a lack of health and wellness, which hampered their ability to work on forward-looking and visionary actions. He applied and was successful in getting the job.

Friday, September 30, 2005, was his last day doing the treaty work. That afternoon, there was a typical community luncheon to celebrate his time in the work and say goodbyes. It was unusual, but not surprising, that Norman wasn't there, despite his involvement in the treaty work. He often did his own thing, and with their tenuous relationship, Joe had learned never to expect him to do the expected. He learned his father was on Vancouver Island, although he didn't know why, as they didn't talk much or often about personal things. Norman had gone to see a doctor.

On the following Monday, October 3, 2005, Joe started working for the Summit. On Tuesday, his brother, who was living at home, called to inform Joe that Norman was sick and was in the hospital. It was initially unclear what was wrong. Norman had never spoken openly about his health with Joe. The reasons he had gone to the doctor the previous week soon became clear: he had lung cancer. It was uncertain at that point how bad it was; Norman was a lifelong smoker, but he hadn't shown any signs of illness until now.

Joe left work in Vancouver and got to Powell River Hospital on the Thursday. By the time he arrived, Norman was in a coma, and the doctors made clear the severity of the issue. His condition was deteriorating quickly, and there was nothing that could be done. On Thanksgiving Monday, October 10, 2005, he passed away at the age of 67. He had never spoken to his children about being sick. He would never see a doctor unless he really had to, and would never talk about his health.

This was the first time Joe had experienced a close connection to cancer. Cancer care was about to become a big issue for him.

When Norman passed, Joe was deeply saddened by the loss. Despite their long and often difficult relationship, he had never really come to know his dad. Since Joe's parents had gone their separate ways a few years earlier, Norman had found his way back home by taking that important Traditional Advisor role in the treaty work. Joe was finally beginning to hear about the tremendous amount of Tla'amin traditional knowledge his father had absorbed while being raised by his great-grandmother.

Joe's initial assignment with the Summit had him seconded to the regional office of Health Canada's First Nations Inuit Health Branch, a position at the executive level responsible for programs and services. This allowed him to form relationships, to gain a better understanding of Health Canada's culture, how it operated as part of the Canadian Public Service, and its relationship with BC First Nations. He remained there for a little more than a year.

This marked the starting point of BC First Nations becoming involved in running the health operations of the federal government, creating the foundations of what would become the First Nations Health Authority six years later.

The job was a significant change for Joe. In his consulting practice, he had been focused on the broad needs of communities. Now he was focused specifically on health and wellness.

His father's death had given Joe a swift introduction to the lack of connection First Nations had with the BC healthcare system—and not in the way he would have wanted or expected. Norman, like so many First Nations people, died having sought out medical help far too late. Almost exactly a year after his death, the father of a good friend also died tragically. Joe spent some time supporting his friend, which triggered his discovery of his own cancer.

On Joe's return to Vancouver from Tla'amin, he went to a soccer practice. He didn't feel himself. He was short of breath and lacked his typical energy level. Because he was engaged in health work, he went to a doctor. He believes that, had he still been doing the treaty work, he would probably have put off seeking help, thinking it was just anxiety and stress. Following many tests and long, anxious waits, the doctors determined he had early-stage colon cancer.

With early detection and colonoscopies, they found the polyps with the cancer cells. He had surgery to remove the cancerous section. Luckily, that took care of it; no radiation or chemo required. He continues to go through regular cancer screening, but so far, so good. Early detection works. Access to care works.

Unfortunately, Joe also lost his mother, Ann, to lung cancer in 2013, at the age of 68. Both his parents were smokers to the end. It was a small part of their lives, something they did to cope with all that they endured as First Nations people.

The Feb. 4, 2021, final report titled "In Plain Sight," on anti-Indigenous racism in the BC healthcare system confirmed that Indigenous people lack sufficient access to family doctors, and 75 percent are more likely to go to an ER than have their own doctor for treatment. Adding a heavy dose of racism to this lack of access, it is no wonder Indigenous health outcomes are worse than those for the general population.

There are examples of very good health care in the system. Just not enough of it. Joe has a family physician in North Vancouver that he met through the birth of his son. Because he was part of the health system, he went to see his doctor.

The ability to access physicians varies depending on various factors, such as whether the patient is in an urban or rural community. The level of care can be very limited in First Nations remote communities. Some communities also experience more extreme racism than others.

Part 8

NAVIGATING A BROKEN SYSTEM

29. Parallel Federal System

"We were trying to figure out how to deal with the health system for First Nations. At that time, we looked at the history and it was pretty depressing. Initially, health was never considered to be a government responsibility, so it wasn't until there was some major calamity that governments got involved." — Ian Potter, federal assistant deputy minister of First Nations and Inuit Health, 2000 to 2008.

John: Eventually the federal government did acknowledge responsibility for Indigenous healthcare but didn't fund it adequately. "It was just a horrible service until after the Second World War," Ian explained. "People came back from the war and wanted a change. There was a kind of revival. The federal government created a new department called Health and Welfare. They took Indian Health out of Indian Affairs and integrated it with the health system. They planned on delivering services."

A parallel structure was introduced including Indian hospitals across the country. But, by the early 1960s it became clear that a separate system for Indian Health would not work. There wasn't enough funding being provided for the parallel system. Of course, creating a separate structure had the result of Indigenous people being denied access to the mainstream system.

The infamous White Paper presented by Trudeau and Chretien in 1969 included a statement that First Nations people should receive health services, like other people, from the organizations most responsible. The provinces hated this idea, as they didn't want to take responsibility for delivering services to First Nations any more than the federal government did. Even when the Supreme Court recognized the First Nations' right to self-government, there were few First Nations willing to take on running their own healthcare.

The challenge, Ian Potter explained, is that "you can't run a health system for 5,000 or 10,000 people. You can barely run a health system for a community of 1 million. It's about economies of scale. This only becomes truer as healthcare becomes more specialized and sophisticated. The liabilities are too significant." Something had to change.

This is one of the issues that eventually led to support for change from Prime Minister Paul Martin, in the form of the Transformative Change Accord, at the Kelowna conference in November 2005.

30. Failings in First Nations Health Care:

1999 Jordan River Anderson

Jordon River Anderson was born in 1999 into the Norway House Cree Nation in Manitoba, with a rare muscular disorder that required him to spend the first two years of his life in hospital. Doctors determined that with specialized medical equipment and training he could then be treated at home instead of in a hospital. Rather than going home, though, he remained in hospital for more than two more years while the governments of Manitoba and Canada argued over who should pay for his at-home care. Jordan passed away in a Winnipeg hospital in 2005 at the age of 5. He never made it home.

2008 Brian Sinclair

Brian Sinclair was a cognitively and physically impaired First Nations man suffering from chronic illness, who needed a wheelchair to get around. Most importantly, he was a human being. He went to a community clinic complaining of abdominal pain and saying he had had no urinary output for the previous 24 hours. The clinic immediately referred him, in writing, to a hospital ER. Just over 30 minutes later, he met with the triage employee at the hospital, who took notes and directed him to wait. He waited for 34 hours, despite his discomfort and vomiting. No medical staff spoke with him, even though non-medical staff and even strangers urged them to do so. When a stranger saw that he was not breathing, he physically grabbed a security guard, and medical staff finally acted. It was too late. Brian Sinclair had been left to die of a treatable condition.

2018 Tania Dick's Aunt

Tania Dick's aunt arrived at a Northern Vancouver Island ER after suffering an unwitnessed fall in her bathroom. She had hit her head and was staggering a little when she entered the hospital. The ER form, when she registered, identified her as being under the influence; they simply assumed she was drunk. She wasn't. Over the course of 18 hours, she was seen by 17 people, all of whom continued to assume she was under the influence of alcohol. Her head injury progressed, and she died without having received treatment. [40]

2020 Joyce Echaquan

Joyce Echaquan, from the Atikamekw Nation, died in a Quebec hospital. Prior to her death she livestreamed her agony on Facebook, screaming in pain while enduring insults and non-treatment from health care workers. They assumed she was coming down from opioids, when in fact she was suffering from a heart condition. When the coroner was asked if the mother of seven would still be alive if she was a white woman, she simply answered, "I think so." She described the situation as "a clear case of systemic racism."

Yet, Quebec Premier François Legault, in ignorance or complete denial, stated that, "There are racist people, but it is not true that the education network, the health care network, have racist systems."[41]

Hearing such stories from Joe and others of mistreatment or non-treatment in the health system confounds me. I have heard some of them before, and I have acknowledged the incidents are unacceptable, but then somehow, they seem to be accepted as "the way it is."

The failings of Canada's health care system when it comes to First Nations go back to Confederation. The provinces were assigned to look after health care for their residents, except for "Indians," for

---

40   https://www.cbc.ca/player/play/1175096899710
Tania Dick is an RN specializing in emergency and Indigenous care.
41   https://www.cbc.ca/news/canada/montreal/
      joyce-echaquan-systemic-racism-quebec-government-1.6196038

whom the federal government retained responsibility. This was the same federal government that was long on a path to get rid of the "Indian problem." First Nations health was never going to get the attention it needed.

On arrival at an emergency room, before there is a proper assessment, First Nations people often hear language to the effect that, "You're drunk, so we don't know what's wrong with you—go sober up before we treat you." Or, "The federal government is responsible for you, so get out of here."

Far too many people are dying in waiting rooms while struggling with a stroke or tumor, while health care providers engage in racial profiling and assume they are impaired.

Each time one of these tragedies makes headlines, the government apologizes and makes promises. But it has continually failed to follow that up with action.

In 2007, the House of Commons passed Jordan's Principle. It established a legislative commitment that Indigenous children are not to have health services withheld while governments fight over who is going to pay. It is tragic that this even needed to be stated.

The Truth and Reconciliation Commission's third of 94 Calls to Action, released in 2015, stated, "We call upon all levels of government to fully implement Jordan's Principle."

In 2016, the Canadian Human Rights Tribunal (CHRT) determined that the child and family services provided to First Nations by the federal government had acted in a discriminatory way.

You would expect that legislation, a TRC report action item, and a ruling by the CHRT would drive compliance, but lawyers representing the federal government continue to put up roadblocks.

"Every step of the way, we've had to take Canada to court to get them to comply with Jordan's Principle." — Cindy Blackstock, executive director of the First Nations Child and Family Caring Society.

The fight continues to be about funding rather than care.

A historic lack of trust also makes it difficult to connect First Nations into the health system, and when treatment is actually received it is too often inadequate and unsafe.

Good dentistry is a vital component of health and wellness. First Nations dental care was also part of the federal government's responsibility, but the program was onerous for dentists. First Nations people would regularly have to get pre-approvals before the dentist could do anything, and dentists wouldn't get their full fee from the federal government. On top of that, the government aggressively audited dentists participating in the program. It was a full-blown cost containment system rather than one designed to look after health. Many dentists refused to deal with the parallel system and would simply turn First Nations people away, saying, "We're not taking new patients under the federal program at this time."

I am happy to say that under the First Nations Health Authority, the dental system became seamless in British Columbia. Access to oral health care for BC First Nations has improved. There are still many dentists whose racist attitudes haven't changed, and relationships remain strained. There is still a lack of trust by both First Nations and dentists, but there is improvement.

Joe found no shortage of opportunities to make improvements in the system, and he committed himself to doing his part to provide better health and wellness for his people.

But he realized it didn't make sense to continue with a system that allowed so many jurisdictional disputes and the resulting gaps in health services. Socio-economic gaps couldn't be solved without taking on jurisdictional and systemically racist structures first.

31. Change of heart

BC Opposition Leader Gordon Campbell's political platform included aggressively challenging the legitimacy of self-government among BC First Nations, including the Nisga'a treaty. When he became premier in 2001, his mantra was that BC was "open for business." He totally disregarded the First Nations agenda, which led to a frustrating lack of progress at the treaty tables.

During his first term, Campbell was attempting to ramp up economic activity, but despite his Liberal Party having gained an unprecedented majority, rights and title disputes involving BC First Nations were causing economic uncertainty. These disputes, many of which ended at the Supreme Court of Canada (as discussed in the earlier section on treaties), were finally starting to be settled in favour of the First Nations.

With most BC First Nations having never signed treaties, the province is in a different environment than most of Canada. Campbell came to recognize that the accommodation of rights and title was a key issue for BC and had to be addressed. Businesses were starting to understand the impact and wanted the economic uncertainty solved.

Campbell realized, to a great extent through relationship work done by Shawn Atleo, BC regional chief at the time, that he was going to have to work with First Nations. He had a complete about-face, a move seldom seen from a politician. In his second term in office, which began in 2005, he became a champion for First Nations causes.

The province finally understood that BC First Nations people had to be recognized as British Columbians, and their unique interest had to be reconciled before the province could move forward economically. Beyond the rights and title issues, Campbell also came to recognize the systemic "less than" treatment that First Nations were receiving. He was influenced by the provincial health officer's 2001 Annual

Report that focused on "The Health and Well-being of Aboriginal People in BC." [42]

The NDP were in power in BC in early 2001 when former provincial health officer Dr. Perry Kendall approached the minister of health in the NDP government. "'The minister asked, 'What is your next report going to be on?' and I said it's going to be on the health of Aboriginal people, and she just said, 'Do you have to?'"

While the minister was supportive of Aboriginal people, this was her way of acknowledging she feared another litany of poor health outcomes would come from it. This was not a new issue, but progress had been slow. When Dr. Kendall began work on the report, the NDP were in government, but by the time it was released, Gordon Campbell's Liberals had formed a new government.

Dr. Kendall further explained, "The report examined the health trends of Status Indigenous people in British Columbia as compared with non-Indigenous people's health outcomes and then looked at the determinants of Indigenous health in BC and compared that with non-Indigenous health determinants."

The report therefore "focused not only on illness, but also determinants like housing, education status, income, culture, and self-determination, etc., and made appropriate recommendations." He added, "while Indigenous health status was worse [than other residents of BC], it was clearly improving, and in the areas where you could make a difference there were clearly gaps with respect to implementable interventions. If one put new policies in place, you could clearly close those gaps. These gaps, through iniquitous social policy, resulted from discrimination and not giving people agency and power over their own resources."

Importantly, Dr. Kendall worked with BC First Nations representatives in preparing the report. "When I was writing the report, there were a number of political First Nations organizations in BC as well as organizations representing Metis and Inuit. They were really, and

---

42   https://www2.gov.bc.ca/assets/gov/health/about-bc-s-health-care-system/office-of-the-provincial-health-officer/reports-publications/annual-reports/phoannual2001.pdf

justifiably, suspicious of having another report written about them: 'That's just what we need. Another colonial report focusing on deficits, with no regard to Indigenous views on health and cultural assets.'

"I said to them, 'I'm writing this report as provincial health officer, but essentially, I have to write it from your perspective, and make it a tool which you could use if you wanted to, respectfully, to improve political and health status of your people.' I stated that the data indicated that the strengths, resilience, and competency of First Nations people and ability to plan, manage, and deliver their health services were key to closing the gaps in health status.

This approach was endorsed and contributed to the report.

"I was committed to meaningful consultation, so it wasn't a report *about* people, but rather it was to be a report that people contributed to and could work with. There were recommendations, and all the Indigenous political organizations endorsed them. I was honoured that that happened, and I believe we created a useful report. When the First Nations Health Authority was then negotiated, there was a plan available and goals adopted that could be used to drive the desired outcomes."

Premier Campbell, after a difficult first term in office, started working with the First Nations Leadership Council that Shawn Atleo brought together, giving Campbell one touch-point to connect with. With the province ready to engage in blue-sky discussions about how things could be different, First Nations leaders wanted to take full advantage of the opportunity.

32. Transformation and Collaboration

Joe: *While I was in my second month at the First Nations and Inuit Health Branch of Health Canada in 2005, the Transformative Change Accord, a historic agreement, was reached between the BC First Nations Leadership Council and the governments of BC and Canada. This agreement represented an incredible opportunity to advance the work between First Nations in BC and the provincial and federal governments, based on the commitment to address the social and economic gaps that exist between First Nations and other British Columbians. This was to be done through an approach that recognized that governments could not act without a workable partnership and meaningful relationship with First Nations people. This was the start of monumental change.*

John: The system was broken, and the only way to fix it was through transformation and collaboration. The effort needed to transform BC First Nations health went well beyond any business challenge I have experienced. Joe's vision and the resilience he had developed through and because of a lifetime of suffering and inequity provided the fuel he needed to lead the transformation of First Nations health and wellness in BC.

There were multiple first-of-their-kind agreements reached on the path of resetting the relationship among the Province of BC, Canada, and First Nations in relation to their rights and title interests. Commitments were made to address social and economic issues, including health, which facilitated the creation of the First Nations Health Council.

There have been, and continue to be, differing philosophies among the three First Nations political organizations in BC. It was the state of First Nations people, including their poor health and wellness, that brought the three together to create the First Nations Leadership Accord and form the First Nations Leadership Council, providing a single voice to negotiate with BC and Canada on socio-economic improvements.

The First Nations Summit. The FNS "provides a forum for First Nations in BC to address issues related to Treaty negotiations as well as other issues of common concern." Joe knew those involved well from the treaty process.

The Union of BC Indian Chiefs. The UBCIC explains that its mandate "is to work towards the implementation, exercise and recognition of our inherent Title, Rights and Treaty Rights and to protect our Lands and Waters, through the exercise and implementation of our own laws and jurisdiction."

The **BC Assembly of First Nations** (AFN). This organization is open to all First Nations. It's described in its vision statement as: "We are proud, progressive and innovative BC First Nations advocating for and implementing our Aboriginal Title, Rights and Treaty Rights through exercising our inherent laws and jurisdiction." "First Nations governments exercising title, rights, and jurisdiction for our lands, resources and peoples in harmony with our customs, languages and laws."

May 2005 - New Relationship Document

Agreement was reached between the First Nations Leadership Council and British Columbia to redevelop relationships based on respect for Aboriginal title and rights and to deal with social and economic inequities. It stretched the boundaries of what was thought possible at the time, toward a shared vision and reconciliation.

The first paragraph from the New Relationship Document made its ambitions clear: "We are all here to stay. We agree to a new government-to-government relationship based on respect, recognition and accommodation of Aboriginal title and rights. Our shared vision includes respect for our respective laws and responsibilities. Through this new relationship, we commit to reconciliation of Aboriginal and Crown titles and jurisdictions. "

November 2005 - Transformative Change Accord

The signing of this agreement took place in Kelowna during the national first ministers and First Nations leadership event that focused on First Nations issues across the country. It was attended by the prime minister, the premiers of all the provinces, territorial leaders, and leaders of national and provincial First Nations organizations in Canada.

As the organizer, Prime Minister Paul Martin demonstrated his deep personal investment in Aboriginal issues. It was at that national meeting that BC Premier Gordon Campbell and BC First Nations leadership were able to get formal support from the national government for the BC First Nations agenda, through the signing of the Transformative Change Accord.

The purpose, as stated in the Accord, was:

"... to achieve the goals of closing the social and economic gap between First Nations and other British Columbians over the next 10 years, reconciling Aboriginal rights and title with those of the Crown, and of establishing a new relationship based upon mutual respect and recognition."

The accord established 10-year commitments in five areas: 1) To improve relationships; 2) To close the gap in education; 3} To close the gap in housing and infrastructure; 4) To close the gap in health; and 5) To close the gap in economic activities.

There was a great deal of work to be done, but the Transformative Change Accord had a big impact, and Premier Campbell's commitment to it was strong. He was just starting his second term. They were going to work together to deliver more.

Of course, nothing involving politics is ever simple. In the new year, Stephen Harper's Conservatives came to power in Ottawa and Paul Martin was out as PM.

There was significant concern around Harper's lack of interest in the First Nations agenda. A lot of what was agreed to in Kelowna with the Paul Martin government at the national level was loosely described by the new Harper government as "agreements written on the back of napkins." The Conservative government had no intention of honouring the results of the Kelowna meeting.

There was indeed a formal document signed by Prime Minister Paul Martin, Premier Campbell, and the First Nations Leadership Council. Campbell remained committed, even though the federal government did not. Canada not living up to its agreements was not new to First Nations.

33. Bilateral Agreement with BC

November 2006 - Bilateral Transformative Change Accord: First Nations Health Plan

Though the Harper government was moving away from the Transformative Change Accord, the provincial government still wanted to demonstrate to BC First Nations that it was serious. The province was committed enough to launch a 10-year bilateral plan on health.

The First Nations Health Plan was the result of focusing on health as one of five streams in the Transformative Change Accord. Of the five, health is the one that has been taken furthest forward.

With the premier pushing hard to get the agreement done, it was written and negotiated on the fly, with his direct involvement. Harmony Johnson worked with Grand Chief Edward John as the Leadership Council lead for health and directly with the Premier's Office. The bilateral health accord was written in two months, encompassing 29 action items pulled together based on work such as the Aboriginal Health Status report prepared by Dr. Perry Kendall's office as the provincial health officer.

The provincial government acknowledged its responsibility to provide health services to First Nations people as British Columbians, regardless of where in BC they lived. Prior to that, based on the Canadian Constitution, the federal government had all responsibility for First Nations health. The accord also recognized that First Nations people needed to be involved in the design and delivery of their health care.

The action items from the bilateral agreement, focused on areas of need as revealed by various health indicators and factors such as life expectancy, diabetes rates, and child obesity.

This bilateral agreement was largely an expression by the BC government that BC First Nations were not invisible. They would be eligible for services like anybody else. They would be involved in the design and delivery of programs for First Nations people, recognizing First Nations' decision-making authority, and their right to self-government and self-determination. It also recognized that people experienced a lot of unsafe interactions in the existing system. This was a positive step to counter a history of First Nations people being *told* what would happen to them. There were still many critics, however, who lacked faith in First Nations' ability to manage their own needs.

Nov 2006 - Tripartite Memorandum of Understanding

Eventually, Health Canada persuaded the federal government to recognize that it had an opportunity to get away from running a parallel health system in BC.

By the time Ottawa finally agreed to get on board, however, it was too late. The province and Leadership Council continued to move forward on a bilateral agreement.

The federal government became reconnected by signing a Memorandum of Understanding (MOU) with the Leadership Council and the Province, agreeing to write a tripartite Health Plan. The pledge in the MOU was that the tripartite plan would be built on the commitments contained in the bilateral plan, and created in six months.

The government of Canada, with Minister Tony Clement on video conference, and Premier Gordon Campbell and the First Nations Leadership Council in attendance, signed that tripartite Memorandum of Understanding (MOU) on November 26, 2006, one day after the release of the Transformative Change Accord: First Nations Health Plan.

These new agreements were groundbreaking. It wasn't the typical scenario, where the government would tell First Nations what was best for them. The Leadership Council was driving the process, covering critical areas including primary care, cultural competency, and increasing the number of First Nations people in health careers.

Joe was already speaking with the First Nations Summit about his next step. With his tripartite negotiation experience and his newly acquired knowledge of federal health programs for First Nations communities, Joe could see the potential. He was talking with Summit political leaders about returning to provide them with the technical leadership he thought would be needed to implement the tripartite plan.

In January 2007, an agreement was reached to end Joe's secondment to Health Canada. He had learned a lot there and got to know people and understood what they were trying to do, but the opportunity to directly support the work of BC First Nations, working together to address the health and wellness of their people, was something he wasn't going to pass up. It was a unique approach and opportunity that did not exist anywhere else in the country.

He was housed at the Summit, but he was in a leadership role working in support of all BC First Nations. Joe uses the term *technical leader* as part of his approach to leading through active engagement. Others might have described him as the leader responsible for execution of these agreements, which is why, once the organization was established as a society, he was given the title of CEO.

34. Taking Action

Joe: *The province needed advice on how to provide better care for First Nations. The bilateral agreement clearly identified that the province's responsibility to provide health services, run hospitals, approve regulations, set standards, etc., had not been diminished. Our team was infusing a First Nations perspective into what already existed. We needed the province fully engaged.*

John: It is one thing to agree to changes at a political level, but fully another to make them a reality. This is where Joe came in.

February 2007 – First Nations Health Council

The first action item was to create a First Nations Health Council. In February 2007, Joe facilitated a session with the First Nations Leadership Council to establish the first iteration of such a body. The Health Council's role would be providing political leadership and advocacy for implementation of the Tripartite First Nations Health Plan. The council was to comprise three Summit representatives, three Union of BC Chiefs representatives, and one BC Assembly of First Nations representative, mirroring the structure of the First Nations Leadership Council. This changed in 2010, when the First Nations Health Council became accountable to First Nations communities and was appointed by five regions, with three representatives per region.

The bilateral agreement's 29 actions were statements agreed to at the political level. Actual implementation of those actions required executive leadership. Joe's job was to establish a team that would work collaboratively to build new partnerships and ensure that space was filled with quality activities, though the provincial health organizations would actually execute the plan. They had the capacity and resources to put the process into action, but historically had had limited capacity to work with First Nations communities.

Provincial health organizations had never really taken First Nations people seriously prior to the bilateral agreement, and now, at least in BC, they needed to work as partners. The provincial health system, with more than 100,000 employees, expends about half of the overall annual provincial budget. Capacity on the First Nations side at that point included the newly formed Health Council, Joe, and a small staff. He was working with staff from the two First Nations political entities. The Summit had a Chiefs' Health Committee, with a staff of about 18. The Union of BC Indian Chiefs also had a social development committee, whose mandate included health. They had some staff there as well who supported the health work.

The objective was to establish a well-rounded partnership with the provincial health system, so they focused on building relationships between First Nations communities and health ministries, health authorities, colleges, professional associations, and educational institutions.

They were engaging with the province and getting to know their systems, as well as starting to work on the principles that would become known as "cultural safety and humility" and developing their concept of health and wellness from a First Nations perspective.

35. Canada Signs on for Transfer

Joe: *We had a significant opportunity in front of us to collectively exercise our right to self-determination over our health and wellness. The opportunity was twofold. First, the transfer of the administration of Health Canada programs and services to a First Nations health organization, through a new health governance partnership, would mean the ability to address First Nations health service issues through First Nations decision-making, with accountability to First Nations through innovation, with a focus on improved services. This was exciting, considering the federal government could not resolve many issues through its colonial framework, which is rigid and only really focused on cost-containment. Secondly, this created the space for a fresh health services partnership, with a much larger provincial health system looking to build new and productive relationships with First Nations to address improved health outcomes. Previous to this, the federal and provincial governments historically did not work well together in support of issues related to First Nations peoples.*

John: When the Tripartite agreement was signed, bringing the First Nations Leadership Council, Canada, and British Columbia into alignment, multiple processes had to be managed:

Partnering with BC Health to implement the 29 action items, and

Establishing the First Nations health governance structure and negotiating the transfer of federal resources to BC First Nations.

Joe and his team started working with the First Nations Health Council to engage with First Nations communities, to get their understanding, and develop consensus on how to work under one umbrella, as well as how the council would fit into a First Nations governance structure.

At the same time, they were negotiating to establish the new health governance partnership in BC, which included transferring federal resources to BC First Nations. Canada's role in First Nations health was to evolve from serving as the designer and deliverer of health programs to a governance partner and funder. The process would move towards First Nations people exercising their own decision-making power over federal resources.

One of Joe's priorities was to build relationships at the strategic and operational levels, in line with political agreements. His strategy was to enhance the work with the Ministry of Health by ensuring that First Nations health and health governance were hard-wired into the ministry processes.

Joe's dad had often told him that he would have to work twice as hard to have success in the "white" world. Building the FNHA was testament to that. Not only did he face the huge challenge of building an organization from scratch—seeing it grow from nothing to more than 900 employees distributed throughout British Columbia—but he was had to do so in a way that ensured it was truly a BC First Nations organization, run by BC First Nations for BC First Nations.

Like all leaders, he needed to:

Set a clear vision and provide motivation;

Build strong partnerships;

Bring in the right skills at the right time;

Develop future leaders;

Build a strong group of advisors; and

Demonstrate success.

In building a First Nations organization, he had an additional focus on:

Implementing a BC First Nations health governance model, exercising the ability to take part in decision-making;

Collaboration among 203 separate entities (First Nations communities/Indian bands) that had been conditioned by colonial policies to work in isolation and were therefore accustomed to making their own decisions. (This is leadership at a level I have never even contemplated);

Building a partnership with a provincial health system that had never been a partner before to First Nations;
Racism and white supremacy;
Cultural safety and humility;
Developing First Nations skills in medical, leadership, and governance roles.

They weren't simply partnering with the provincial government and transferring services over from the federal government. They were breaking down colonial barriers to fill the major gap in health care quality faced by First Nations in BC. In many ways, this was the continuation of a battle Joe had been fighting his entire life.

They were building an organization that would represent all 203 First Nations and give them a voice. They had to work to ensure that no one got left behind.

36. Gathering Wisdom for a Shared Journey

Joe: *The goal of settler colonialism was to get rid of the Indian problem. "Divide and conquer" was an approach taken by government that was reflected through legislation that divided nations into small Indian bands and program policies that pitted the small bands against one another to secure scarce funding. Therefore, collaboration was not straightforward for First Nations, thanks to the impact of this colonial legislation and policies. Nations were all at a different level in terms of building their capacity and going through decolonization.* "Gathering Wisdom for a Shared Journey" *was about bringing our First Nations together to begin a conversation about working collectively to address common concerns, in the belief that we are truly "better together" and to ensure that "No one gets left behind."*

Gathering Wisdom. Leonard George at the podium.

Gathering Wisdom blanketed by Nike N7 team

John: Joe and his team, under the "better together" theme, worked at trying to bring everyone to one table. If they were to succeed as a First Nations organization for First Nations, they needed to build support and leadership at the community level. A BC First Nations health governance structure would form the foundation upon which everything would be built.

Collaboration isn't easy, but it is the traditional First Nations approach. Jody Wilson-Raybould, in her book *'Indian' in the Cabinet*, described it this way:[43]

"For many Indigenous peoples, decision-making is communitarian and consensus-based, though there are many differences and distinctions between peoples and nations in how decision-making operates. We are always working to build that consensus from which

---

43 *'Indian' in the Cabinet* (pp. 36-37). Jody Wilson-Raybould. HarperCollins Publishers. Kindle Edition.

a decision will emerge. Individuals do not decide, nor do they have the authority to decide. The spark of truth comes from everyone contributing, sharing, and building the best decision together. Almost every Indigenous environment that I have been in—whether it was gatherings of hundreds of Chiefs, around my small Band Council table, in community halls, or at the executive of the AFN—at the end of the day, striving for consensus was the paramount ethic."

As I write about the various stages in the development of First Nations health, I refer to the overall organization rather than to Joe as a leader. I do this with respect for Joe's humility. I mention this so that, as you read through this account of the growth of the organization, you might pause and recognize the level of leadership he provided. You will also hear this when I quote others Joe worked with.

Having a vision nobody else can see does no good. The role of the First Nations Health Council was to establish the vision from a political perspective, with BC First Nations as well as the federal and provincial governments. Joe's role was to work with political leaders to shape that vision and then provide leadership to the newly forming First Nations health team, to work with the province as full partners. The task was to breathe life into the vision by putting into operation initiatives that, with everyone striving together, would transform the health system.

First Nations from across the province came together in highly involved engagements called the "Gathering Wisdom for A Shared Journey" sessions. All the chiefs, as political leads, plus technical leads—some 500 or so people—participated in this provincial dialogue. These were First Nations meetings with ceremony, with government representatives brought in to share their piece.

Joe helped organize the first Gathering Wisdom in 2007, but he missed it while recovering from cancer surgery. It was the beginning of what would become a ten-year conversation on health, based on the model spelled out in the Transformative Change Accord: First Nations Health Plan. This dialogue would be an essential part of the BC First Nations Health Governance Structure.

The two- to three-day Gathering Wisdom sessions were ground-breaking meetings specifically to discuss health and wellness issues and priorities, with delegates meeting in plenary and in regional caucuses to advance issues. As the sessions evolved, the conclusions of regional and community meetings were brought forward to shape the agenda. Previously, at regular political gatherings, the chiefs' agenda had been too full to devote more than limited time to issues of health and wellness. It was critical to ensure leaders that their concerns would be heard to help shape the mandate.

From the beginning, in meetings with chiefs, councillors, and health directors, there was a concerted effort to focus on participants first as human beings, being mindful of the role played by politics. This meant beginning gatherings with culture and ceremony. In addition, preventative wellness checks were made available to leaders via a health fair during Gathering Wisdom meetings, as well as the opportunity to participate in health and wellness activities delivered by First Nations providers.

Political work and strategies to address settler colonialism were needed to bring the chiefs together. But once everyone was in the room, their interactions were as First Nations people. The gatherings were about building consensus around First Nations health and wellness, through meaningful dialogue as human beings about fundamental issues affecting real people, such as cancer, diabetes, or mental illness—and doing it through a First Nations lens.

Chiefs and leaders came together not only to bring their perspectives, community by community, but also to work together as nations and as a collective of nations. This collaboration would be the foundation of a new health governance partnership with the federal and provincial governments, putting primary decision-making in the hands of BC First Nations.

Guests were invited to share their own stories and journeys from Alaska, Hawaii, and New Zealand. They offered inspiring examples that helped fire the imagination of the BC participants.

Doing this work allowed Joe to spend time with and learn from Indigenous people from other countries. He, in turn, was invited to travel and speak at various forums. Indigenous people in various parts of the world were working through their own unique frameworks, but for Joe what stood out in these encounters was the resiliency of Indigenous peoples, who all continue to battle with their colonial histories.

The US is well ahead of Canada on creating space for Indigenous nations to take control of their own matters. In the 1980s, the US passed legislation that allowed tribes to organize and take over administration and authority in health, education, and social development. BC First Nations political leaders, Health Canada, and others travelled to Alaska to learn more about the Alaska Tribal Consortium, a collaborative approach among Native Alaskan political leadership, and to discuss how it has organized Native Alaska Regional Health Corporations. In Alaska, there are about 230 tribes in some very remote areas covering a large geography—a relatable situation for First Nations in BC. Their process has allowed them to work collaboratively as tribes addressing their own health needs, including developing their own capable leaders to run their health system. They are 20 to 30 years ahead of BC First Nations with this opportunity to work together and make their own decisions.

Joe enjoyed going to New Zealand, where the Māori treaty provides for representation in the political process and federal government. The Māori have made great progress in retaining their language and culture, yet their colonial history still results in health challenges. The situation in Australia was different, as Indigenous people there continue to advance their health and wellness issues as part of a broader agenda seeking formal recognition by the federal government.

To support BC First Nations' participation, community engagement hubs were established. This initiative invited First Nations to determine for themselves how they wanted to organize working together. Resources were provided to support work in communication, collaboration, and planning. First Nations have spent enough of their colonial history being told what to do; they needed to define for themselves what meaningful relationships were and how they should work. Community engagement hubs evolved to become part of the regional caucus process, to work with their respective regional health authority service providers.

There were two main streams of work. Bringing BC First Nations together under one governance structure required many discussions among chiefs and leaders to get them to a common place. At the same time, it was essential to do significant work with provincial health services. Joe worked with the First Nations Health Council to create a health governance committee to address political work with the chiefs, while the council continued to oversee work to improve provincial services.

The Governance Committee, given the politicized nature of the dialogue, ended up being chaired by three people, one appointed by each of the three First Nations political organizations: Grand Chief Doug Kelly, representing the BC Assembly of First Nations; Grand Chief Ed John, representing the Summit; and Kukpi7 (Chief) Wayne Christian, representing the Union of Indian Chiefs. The committee eventually had 30 additional members, who were tasked with creating the governance structure and building consensus on it—a very difficult task on a committee of 33.

From the beginning, the goal was to separate business from politics, knowing that would be a challenge. Joe supported the political work with the committee and provided the capacity required to carry out their work. They would focus on getting people into the room to discuss the opportunities and political differences and work to achieve consensus.

Over the course of four years, there were some 140 community engagements at local, First Nation, regional and provincial levels. There were many meetings dealing with issues, answering questions, addressing fears, and creating opportunities.

The governance discussions were a lead-in to the transfer of federal services, but the job was more than taking over existing federal programs. They were building an institution that would give BC First Nations control and allow them to redesign the policy to be one their people could be proud of, that embraced their traditions and teachings and was culturally safe.

They were establishing governance that gave First Nations people the right to make spending decisions and offer quality service delivery. They were introducing a First Nations style of decision-making. Both governments realized there were parts of the existing healthcare system didn't work well for First Nations and which needed to be addressed together. This required the province's commitment to First Nations' governance and recognition of their right to self-determination, as guaranteed in the Constitution.

The public service's definition of *health* was too narrow for First Nations. The program focused primarily on hospitals, treatment, and disease, whereas First Nations were thinking holistically, with wellness and prevention part of the mix.

Katie Skelton, FNHA: "Joe never veered from health and wellness. It was the same when we would talk about mental health. He was very adamant that we say 'mental health and wellness.'"

Joe was committed to good governance, long-term sustainability, and proper management of resources. When the tripartite agreement was signed, both governments had agreed to commit funding, but for the first three to four years, the First Nations Health Council were only partially and inconsistently funded, despite signed agreements. Eventually that got sorted out, but they did have to manage the money in a way that could stretch it out if needed. If they had spent it all, they would have been out of business in year two. Joe believed strongly in wise spending and accountability, as would be expected from everyone else. They had a big agenda, and if the spending request wasn't for something within their focus, they wouldn't just push the money out. They were doing it in a smart way.

If the health society received funding, there was consideration of what should go to communities to support their involvement, but the overall mandate was to build something lasting. The mantra was, "Good governance is sustainability." Seven generations since first contact, BC's First Nations were still here. They couldn't do anything now to jeopardize that.

Ian Potter, the assistant deputy minister and chief negotiator for the federal government, described Joe's plan:

"It was his new idea of partnerships. He talked about reciprocal accountability. Joe had this notion that we had to find a way to coexist. Under Joe's form of partnership, you not only have accountability to your own people, but you also have accountability to your partner's goals.

"People had a lot of respect for him because he was very ethical. He was dogged and determined and sometimes a pain in the ass. He had amazing attention to detail."

Joe's dogged determination came up several times in interviews, as did that depiction of him as a "pain in the ass." It was always said with a chuckle, but I now understand it, having had my own experience with his unrelenting ways.

37. CEO

Joe: *It was a great honour to be considered and given the title of CEO of the First Nations Health Society, the organization that ultimately became the First Nations Health Authority. The board of this new society had the responsibility of choosing the CEO. None of them had been involved in the work up to that point in time, so they were not familiar with my work. If it wasn't me they wanted to run their organization, they would need to let me know. Until then, I was the operational lead for the work and was doing my best to contribute to the development and implementation of a strategy to build something that would make the world better for our people everywhere. If my work was good enough, they would tell me.*

John: Patiently waiting for someone else to determine what Joe's entitlement was is a reflection of his history. Everywhere he had worked, he just trusted that he would be paid fairly. Unlike most CEOs, he had not grown up with any sense of privilege or entitlement.

In 2009, the organization moved from being an informal network of the three First Nations political organizations to becoming more formalized as the First Nations Health Society, a nonprofit society whose main purpose was to be the operational arm of the First Nations Health Council, which had the responsibility of appointing the board of directors, which in turn would appoint a chief executive officer (CEO).

Joe had been executive lead in the work, but it was unclear if the board, which was not directly familiar with his contributions, would be confident in Joe as CEO if they simply inherited him. To support this process, Joe engaged an HR consultant to evaluate himself. He proactively had a full 360-degree review done of his own performance, which included conversations with all the partners and primary stakeholders. The consultant presented a confidential report to the board, without Joe being present, that included a lot of positive feedback, and that's how he was chosen. Things were moving quickly. Joe had won the competition way back in 2005 to be director of health programs. Now, four years later, he was the CEO, and it was about to become a whole new ball game.

There were good people on the board, both Indigenous and non-Indigenous, some with experience in healthcare, others with government experience, and others with First Nations environments.

Work was well underway to implement both the Transformative Change Accord: First Nations Health Plan and the Tripartite Health Plan. Over time, after a few tests were thrown his way, the board got to know Joe and his leadership, and he developed a positive working relationship with them.

It would still be four more years before all services were transferred and a couple of years before the framework agreement was approved by the chiefs, so there was plenty of work ahead.

38. Consensus

Joe: *Consensus-building was fundamental to how First Nations governments worked in the past, before the imposed democratic system of chief and council under the Indian Act. Decisions back then were made when everyone had an opportunity to engage in the dialogue and contribute to the final decision. Once the decision was made, then everyone would work to uphold it. To work toward consensus in this process, many dialogue sessions were held with all First Nations. Sometimes at the community level, at a nation level, at a regional level, or at a provincial level. The conversations were meaningful and engaging. First Nations across the province were in many different places depending on the impact of their experiences with settler colonialism. Questions and fears were raised and, through dialogue, turned into opportunity. A lot of good work was done, in culturally appropriate ways, to achieve a level of consensus that would provide the mandate to move forward collectively. It was an incredible, unprecedented demonstration of First Nations self-determination in action.*

September 2010 - Basis for a Framework Agreement presented for consideration and agreement from the chiefs.

John: Creating the BC First Nations health governance partnership involved negotiating a process by which the Framework Agreement would gain political alignment from the chiefs ahead of finalizing the legal agreements. Coming to an agreement among chiefs was an incremental step toward confirming what would be included in the Framework Agreement.

Information was shared to help First Nations leaders imagine what the framework could look like and allow them to provide feedback.

The focus was on helping them see a future that could be achieved by working on things together, emphasizing the benefits at a local level while being clear about the issues and challenges.

May 2011 – Consensus Paper and Tripartite Framework Agreement

At the Gathering Wisdom meeting in May 2011, a Consensus Paper was presented that included the accumulated feedback from regional and subregional caucus meetings over the past four years, containing the response from various First Nations as well as documents confirmed by chiefs, leaders, and senior health professionals. At that session, motions were passed, resolutions drawn up, and votes taken confirming support for the Framework Agreement.

The Framework Agreement specified a series of specific smaller agreements to be negotiated with Health Canada to address the many elements of the federal programs and services that were being transferred.

An important component of the consensus document was that it confirmed the community-driven directives under which the FNHA, the First Nations Health Council, and First Nations health directors would operate:

Directive #1: Community-Driven, Nation-Based
Directive #2: Increase First Nations Decision-Making and Control
Directive #3: Improve Services
Directive #4: Foster Meaningful Collaboration and Partnership
Directive #5: Develop Human and Economic Capacity
Directive #6: Be Without Prejudice to First Nations Interests
Directive #7: Function at a High Operational Standard

Several people I spoke to who worked with Joe said the initial list contained only six directives. Joe introduced No. 7, knowing that a high operating standard was critical to building a sustainable organization.

The consensus document also stated the understanding that regional caucuses would carry on, lining up with the BC Health regional structure to provide support and promote health and wellness in a community-driven, nation-based way.

Joe sees the 2011 decision as the most important self-determination decision ever made in British Columbia. Never had all the communities agreed to go in one direction before. They had inspired themselves to work together. They were making hard decisions, but they were *making* them rather than having someone make them for them.

Allison Twiss, former regional advisor, FNHA: "Joe never did anything without making sure everyone's viewpoint was or could be heard. He was skillful at being wholly representative. This is why he was so trusted. No one was left behind; no community was left behind. Only a cohesive movement together would ensure this journey was successful, as demonstrated by the near-consensus vote taken by BC First Nations' leadership at Gathering Wisdom IV, marking BC First Nation communities' decision to move forward and assume governance and technical leadership of Health Canada, BC Region. This was a historic event for BC First Nations. Unprecedented.

"Because of Joe's leadership, his team made possible what was thought not possible. He carved out a future and space of precedence to make all things possible for BC First Nation individuals, families, communities, and subsequent generations.

"There is, and has been, no other leader like Joe."

Part 9

THEY DIDN'T THINK IT COULD BE DONE

39. Transfer

Joe: *An entire regional office of the federal government had never been transferred to a First Nations organization before. This was unprecedented, incredibly complex, and would require an effective partnership between all parties to support its success. The transfer included all federal services and functions, as well as the staff and infrastructure used to support the delivery of those services and functions. Leading up to the transfer, I knew many of the federal employees from the regional office from my time working there. Many of the staff came over excited about the new opportunity to work in a First Nations health and wellness organization, while others were very skeptical and were never going to be happy. It was a time where most had limited options, so they had to come across. It was clear that we would need to do the best we could to build workable relationships, to make the transition as smooth as possible. In the end, with all the complexity and drama, I realized that, in working with our partners, we did our best to meet the initial success measures for the transfer. On October 1, 2013, the sun came up as usual and transfer day was here, and it was successful.*

John: As negotiations were ongoing with the federal government, there was an economic downturn, and the government of Canada was in cost-cutting mode across the country; this included some layoffs. BC First Nations negotiated to protect the regional budget as an essential element for the agreement, as they would not support a deal where resources were being reduced before agreement was reached. This also provided protection for Health Canada employees in the region that were destined to be transferred to the First Nations Health Authority. This was positive in that individual jobs were protected, and it ensured the Health Authority didn't lose all the people it would need to run its programs post-transfer. However, the deficit reduction approach by Canada also meant the Health Canada employees had little to no options for moving anywhere else in the Canadian government. If people didn't believe in what was being done, or wanted to stay working for Canada, they had nowhere else to go.

The first meeting that brought together 200 established Health Canada employees and 100 First Nations Health employees was critical to overcoming the clash of cultures to create a cohesive team. The First Nations and non–First Nations work cultures were different. Many in these groups had once served in roles where they were on opposite sides of the table, addressing conflict. On top of this, some Health Canada employees weren't happy about becoming part of a First Nations organization. Others simply didn't believe it could be successfully run by First Nations.

Allison Twiss, former regional advisor, FNHA: "I remember the first FNHS and Health Canada BC Region gathering where we all came together. It was more of a chunky mosaic than a blending of keen, passionate, First Nations health champions with government employees. Joe showed up to the event and set the tone intentionally by being dressed more casually than usual. This symbolic action took the tension in the room down a level and invited a more welcoming and human approach. One of the senior directors from Health Canada, dressed in a suit and tie, came up to Joe in front of the conference room and gave him permission to cut his tie off—Joe literally took a pair of scissors and did so. The director expressed intent to join the BC First Nations' wellness journey, and his interest in making the commitment to join Joe's team at the First Nations Health Authority. This was a symbolic act of leadership on his part, as, while some of his colleagues chose to join the journey, many quickly fled their roles, as they did not see themselves, nor their passion, in the work; some, worse, expressed that they didn't believe the FNHA could be successful.

"This day, one of us all coming together, really set the tone— everyone was welcome, everyone's choices would be unconditionally accepted and understood; and yet, if you stayed, there was a needed coming together of spirit—and of course, Joe set this tone with light and humour at heart, and always relationally oriented. Kindness and compassion, balanced with the needed discipline and firmness that our joint task called for."

* * *

In October 2011, the formal Framework Agreement was signed with BC and Canada, as always with cultural aspects and ceremony. This paved the way for further negotiation and developing the operational infrastructure to transfer people and systems over to the new entity.

There were more operational agreements to come, involving transferring infrastructure, union issues, HR issues, and budgets. As the last of the political agreements, the Framework set out responsibilities of the partners and confirmed the transfer of responsibilities.

May 2012 – First Nations Health Authority

At the May 2012 Gathering Wisdom V, BC First Nations officially decided that the First Nations Health Society would become the First Nations Health Authority (FNHA). At this point, Joe could start establishing his senior team formally.

Building a community-driven organization created some challenges in this regard. Joe knew strong leadership was needed, but not a top-down hierarchy that First Nations would perceive as an "Ivory tower." There wasn't much time to put this in place and decide the particulars of how the structure would be run and what the work would be.

The FNHA was no longer responsible just as the operations arm of the Health Council; it would now be taking on service responsibilities for First Nations health and wellness across the province. The team needed to create an organization appropriate to First Nations, not one like the federal government. Executing this from a leadership/ management perspective was one of the greatest challenges.

Unlike the provincial work, which meant working in partnership to improve provincial health care for First Nations, this was a complete administrative transfer. The initial emphasis was on making sure things kept running afterwards.

July-October 2013 – Transfer of responsibility for delivering First Nations health programs

The following excerpt from the federal government website in October 2021, describing the state of the Canadian health system, provides a good indication of what Joe and his team were up against:

"With respect to health care for First Nations, Inuit and Métis Nation, the federal, provincial and territorial levels share some degree of jurisdiction. The Canadian health system is a complex patchwork of policies, legislation and relationships."[44]

Even the Canadian government recognized the inefficiencies of their own First Nations health care system. The last sentence could be updated to include: "but it is far better in British Columbia."

Lynn Stevenson, BC assistant deputy health minister – Speaking at the Quality Council a few years after the transfer took place, Stevenson reflected on how much had changed. "When I talk to my colleagues across the country, they are gobsmacked by the work that is going on here—the cutting-edge work that the FNHA has done and is doing. I think sometimes we take it for granted. I guess I am here to tell you we should never take that for granted. I spend a fair amount of time talking to my provincial counterparts, and they are continually wondering in awe how we got here."

John: On transfer day the switch was flipped, and the design, management and delivery of First Nations health programming was in the hands of the First Nations Health Authority. A team of 300 was running everything that Canada used to do, either with their

---

44   https://www.sac-isc.gc.ca/eng/1626810177053/1626810219482

own systems or with a hodgepodge of federal technology until it was possible to transition away from it. It took almost two years to get that working comfortably. BC continues to be the only province doing this.

They were now a service organization, and at first their focus was on running the transferred services as seamlessly as possible. They had to keep the plane flying while moving toward transformational change with a new set of pilots.

The Health Authority had taken on a substantial budget, with accountability for the health and well-being of First Nations people, both on and off reserves. Through partnership discussions about hard-wiring First Nations health into senior-level discussions within the Provincial Health System, the deputy health minister asked Joe to join the BC Health Leadership Council. This was the deputy minister's strategic table with the CEOs of all the provincial health authorities. Participating gave Joe an opening to bring a First Nations lens to broader discussions about health services.

The organization worked on building regional capacity to support its work with the province and provide much-needed services to First Nations people that previously had been substandard or unavailable. Many initiatives were centred on wellness and cultural safety and humility, with many new leaders in new roles.

Simply put, there was a lot to do. Joe no longer was able to speak to everyone at the level he would like. As CEO, he was spending a lot of time putting out fires, addressing issues and problems coming at him, and driving the strategy and vision for health system transformation from a First Nations health perspective.

The organization grew more quickly than he would have liked, and not everything was done perfectly. The Health Authority needed to refine and navigate through competing needs at the operational level. It wasn't long before Joe was running an organization of 900 people, still using the original model of funding from the federal government based on what it had previously been spending directly.

Provincial Health Officer Perry Kendall had recognized in his 2001 report that "you can spend your money a lot better if you gave it to the people, let them govern their services, let them deliver their services, train them to deliver the services, and be a partner in this endeavor." This was coming to fruition.

Mary Campling, former CFO, First Nations Health Authority. "Joe was all about the longer-term goal of better health outcomes for First Nations people in BC, whether they were in community on reserve or in urban areas. I think it was really difficult for [Joe], as he decided to change some leaders and people who had been there from the beginning, but he recognized that as the organization evolved, he needed his leadership team to evolve. He made some tough decisions. The other was the need for fiscal accountability. I told Joe that he is the only CEO that I would ever say that I was completely transparent with about all the money. I had the utmost faith he would use the knowledge very strategically, and he did."

40. A Higher Standard

Joe: *The First Nations Health Authority was always going to be held to a higher standard as a First Nations organization delivering the same functions that the federal government did previously. Like any change of this magnitude, there were growing pains. However, as expected, because this was a First Nations organization, there were many doubters who were hoping, or expecting, that we would fail. People in society expect First Nations peoples to fail, and believe that we don't belong in these spaces. Some even purposely took actions to undermine the work we were doing. Like my dad had always said to me, we needed to be twice as good.*

John: The FNHA drew in people from various organizations, which led to some challenges, particularly as the team was building a first-of-its-kind organization. It was going to be challenging. Not everyone would last in the work, and that was okay.

Some employees transferred in from the federal government. Some hires didn't work out as well as others, because they couldn't get their thinking aligned. Others found success. A lot of changes were made. Joe eventually replaced much of his senior executive team, ensuring he had a group that could build the FNHA to a point of stability.

I admire how Joe approached this. He was not a hero CEO who thought he could take everything on himself. He recognized the need to build a team that could together fulfill the vision.

Some people hoped this new reality wouldn't change the status quo, but it did. It was a challenge to build trust, and there were issues to work through, as a few of the 200 Health Canada employees were not happy to be leaving to work for a First Nations–run organization. Joe made it clear that, while everyone had an opportunity, some might find it wasn't the work for them.

Davis Mckenzie, former FNHA employee in communications:
"We had Health Canada employees leaking documents to the National Post, insinuating that the transfer was not well grounded, or being looked after, and this is before the transfer took place. Joe, working with Leonard George, used First Nations teachings and diplomacy to make it work. You keep people safe while doing the work, but people needed to reach their own outcomes.

"I think the biggest thing was that it was some people's fundamental, societal belief that we couldn't do it, and we certainly couldn't do it better. It goes back to a really strong societal structural stereotype."

Danielle Searancke, former FNHA employee: "Joe has a very inspirational leadership style. Your mind can be very busy, and you don't know where you are going, but one conversation with Joe and he would ground you. He brings the spirit back into what you are doing. That's his gift.

"When I first started and was trying to get meetings for Joe in Ottawa and Victoria, it was like a circus. I was trying to get on people's agenda, and we were forever getting bumped. By the time I left, they were calling us to try to initiate discussions. Joe's reputation got us a needed seat at the table."

Allison Twiss, former regional advisor, FNHA: "Joe was always a partner to each BC First Nation community, to each family, to each individual in the work. Roles were clear and aligned with the highest vision, and in the highest level of respect, Joe invited and held people to their commitments, professional accountabilities, and their own personal sense of what was right. Joe built a rich tapestry where all partners in the work had a role they were called to execute— First Nation communities, the urban community, federal and provincial governments, health authority boards, operational leadership, and technicians/practitioners, etc. .... He referred to the work as the hard-wiring of the system, because for true health and wellness to occur and be lasting, it would take a systems approach, involving everyone. The work belonged to everyone.

The FNHA is a partnership. About a third of the workforce are BC First Nations, and it provides an opportunity to open doors and create further career opportunities for BC First Nations people, which will help strengthen their families. ...

"If you haven't managed a large group of people, it may be difficult to grasp just how difficult Joe's task was. He was bringing together lifelong bureaucrats, some visionary, some not; with BC First Nations governance leadership (with diverse and unique interests); with seasoned health directors (many chronically underfunded by Canada); with health authorities' operational leadership and boards (constantly turning over); with professional colleges, and with his own FNHA team. At the same time, Joe had the navigational eye to ensure the common health and wellness destination for the 203 BC First Nations, each with their own unique culture and traditional knowledge system driving the work, and each critical to honour. The task was monumental, yet it was achieved. Joe met it with success."

41. Partnering with The Provincial Health Officer

Joe: *To truly implement First Nations health governance on behalf of all First Nations, we were in a position to be involved in the governing of First Nations data and measuring our own health and wellness. This would enable the FNHA to lead the work with First Nations, to report on the health and wellness status of our population, and begin to address the stereotypes and misperceptions that persist in our settler colonial society. The provincial health officer was instrumental in shaping the action items in the 2006 TCA: First Nations Health Plan and was an essential partner to support the implementation of this approach.*

John: The team was focused on building strength-based capacity. In their early work with Perry, there were discussions about bringing on an Aboriginal physician advisor role, for which Dr. Evan Adams was eventually hired.

Evan is a source of pride to his community; he has experienced tremendous individual success and popularity through his acting career, and he is also held in high esteem as a doctor.

As part of the Framework Agreement, the position of deputy provincial health officer with responsibility for First Nations/Aboriginal health was established; it was a role that would have real authority and not just an advisory capacity. Evan evolved into this role.

Later, a working partnership was created between the chief medical officer of the First Nations Health Authority and the provincial health officer. The First Nations Health Authority established its own team of medical officers for BC First Nations. This team works alongside the provincial health officers to advance a First Nations–driven population health agenda, thus building capacity to lead and tell their own story on health and wellness in these communities.

Evan was awarded the position of FNHA's chief medical officer through an open process. Joe made sure not to participate in that choice because he was from the same community and wanted to avoid any perception of favouritism. The chief medical officer would not only become the lead public health spokesperson for BC First Nations but also lead the partnership with the Office of the Provincial Health Officer.

Evan was perfectly situated by the time he joined the team. He worked with Joe's support and advice to establish his team and take on the authority of his position, representing the First Nations as their public health voice, something they did not have until then.

The strong relationship with the provincial health office continued through the ten years that followed the signing of the Transformative Change Accord in 2006. Then it was time to renew the commitment. Knowing Perry Kendall was approaching retirement, Joe challenged Perry to work with Evan to come up with an expanded indicator agenda for the following 10 years—one that wasn't just about indicators of sickness but would also focus on First Nations wellness. The two agreed and began the work. After his retirement, Perry contracted to the FNHA to continue the work, ensuring there were people at the table to help meld the traditional and Western approaches for this new set of health and wellness indicators. In addition, the Provincial Health Office started gathering First Nations community-based indicators of health.

Perry Kendall, former BC provincial health officer: "Joe challenged us to come up with broader health goals which would reflect the Indigenous concept of wellness, which is so much more holistic than our focus on hospitals. We came up with measures that could tell us whether we were being successful in changing our approach to Indigenous patients. How many trained Indigenous physicians and nurses in each health authority? How many people are taking cultural sensitivity training? Specific Indigenous-based surveys.

"The other board members were very good at letting you know if you were being racist or stupid or ignorant. Joe would then come in and do the work with you to do what needed to be done. It was a good partnership."

Part 10

BUILDING A FIRST NATIONS ORGANIZATION

42. First Nations Knowledge and Teachings

Joe: *To successfully build a First Nations health and wellness organization that all First Nations in BC could be proud of, it had to be grounded in our knowledge and teachings. To be disciplined in First Nations health governance, it was essential to begin this work with the knowledge and teachings of the host nations where the FNHA head office was located. To begin this, I reached out to Qut-same—Leonard George, Knowledge Keeper, chief, and highly respected leader from the Tsleil-Waututh Nation. Working with Qut-same was a real gift that helped me grow as a First Nations leader. We spent a lot of time together, talking about First Nations and Indigenous teachings that he had experiences with, from his many years and travels, and their application to the work at hand for First Nations peoples. Qut-same would talk about being lifelong learners and of seeking knowledge from Knowledge Keepers, from First Nations communities and from spiritual leaders from around the world. He would tell me that he was only halfway through his learning journey, which illustrates just how much I still had to learn.*

Joe at FNHA/UBC Cancer Chair announcement. With Leonard George on Joe's left, UBC President Santo Ono on his right.

John: Early in the process of building the FNHA, Joe brought in Qut-same to help with establishing the appropriate organizational culture. He was an inspirational First Nations leader who had a reputation for working effectively for the rights of his people and creating collaborative partnerships with the non–First Nations world. The Tsleil-Waututh ancestral lands include areas of what is now known as North Vancouver and Vancouver, which made it necessary for the Tseil-Waututh to do business and build partnerships with the world around them. He was building partnerships grounded in Tsleil-Waututh teachings and knowledge. They were based on mutual respect and trust, and Joe still sees that as the only way to move forward. He was committed to building a First Nations organization they could be proud of.

Qut-same had dedicated his life to seeking knowledge and doing his best to live the values and teachings of the Tseil-Waututh people.

Joe asked him to join the FNHA family as someone that could provide cultural teachings and guidance to help shape an FNHA organizational culture appropriate to a First Nations–owned and –run health and wellness organization. Qut-same found the work appealed to him, as he shared the vision of improving the health of First Nations people. He would remind everyone of their responsibility to be the best person they could be every day—and to be their authentic selves. Following this at the FNHA became an individual job responsibility, as well as the collective role.

Qut-same demonstrated his commitment to the health governance work and his support for the FNHA family when, at a staff gathering, he graciously adopted the FNHA family into his Tak'aya Wolf Clan. This was a generous gift from him, his family, and the Tsleil-Waututh people. Being adopted into the Tak'aya Wolf Clan meant that the FNHA family had a common First Nations identity. With that identity came the responsibility to live the teaching and values of the clan while in service to all BC First Nations. It was an important recognition to be honoured in this manner from a great and respected leader. The Tak'aya Wolf Clan teachings and values were now fundamental to establishing the First Nations culture for the FNHA. They were shared with the FNHA, to guide the family in how they embraced their work. These teachings and values gave the FNHA family what they needed to be successful as a transformative First Nations health and wellness organization.

Around the time of the transfer, Joe came up with the idea of having his senior leadership team, together with Qut-same, learn to sing the "Coast Salish Anthem" in preparation for opening the upcoming Gathering Wisdom forum. The leadership team was a mix of people—not all First Nations, and not all from BC. It seemed appropriate to have Qut-same teach the song to the team. The anthem had been his father's—Chief Dan George's—prayer song, which had been adopted by the Coast Salish Nations as their anthem. It was another honour for Qut-same to share the anthem with the FNHA, and a great opportunity for for the senior leadership team to practice humility and learning. At first, some struggled to get it, but it was good fun for all. And what a special gift to learn it directly from Qut-same. The anthem became a big part of who they were; each Monday morning, teams across the FNHA would gather and hold a circle to start the week off in a good way by grounding themselves with the anthem. It became a component of "being our best."

Other First Nations teachings were incorporated into the FNHA. With a footprint that extended across the province, each regional team would leverage the help of Knowledge Keepers for local First Nations. Spirit baths and sweats were among many cultural/spiritual practices incorporated by the FNHA family across the province. For example, with offices in West Vancouver and Downtown Vancouver, it was common to hold spirit baths for cleansing at Ambleside Beach, by the mouth of the Capilano River. Having FNHA family members take time from the day for spirit baths, guided by a Squamish Nation Knowledge Keeper, Syexwaliya, reinforced the message—for both First Nations and non–First Nations team members—that you need to look after yourself in order to look after someone else.

After Leonard George passed, Joe brought in Sulksun – Shane Point, a Musqueam Knowledge Keeper, to provide cultural guidance.

43. Finding a Place at the Leadership Table

Joe: *The health governance partnership was new to both the federal and provincial governments, and it was essential to nurture the relationship to keep the work advancing as well as possible. The federal government had existing relationships with First Nations, but these were based on principles rooted in settler colonialism. From a health perspective, the province and First Nations didn't have much of a relationship, because First Nations health had been a federal responsibility. However, developing the health partnership with the province represented a real opportunity for transformation. Reciprocal accountability is an important aspect of a good partnership. This includes not only doing our best for one another in nurturing the partnership but also being clear about what we expect from the other. Once that is understood, accountabilities can be defined.*

John: As much as one can try to build trust, what you are really are trying to create is a common understanding, each getting to know the other better. This is why Joe would always talk about governance before health care. it was important to establish parameters with the province and with Canada, to understand each as a separate entity. This was prior to UNDRIP and the Truth and Reconciliation Report, so it could be a challenge to gain this understanding.

Katie Skelton, FNHA, Anishinaabe, Ojibwe. Member of Henvey Inlet First Nation: "Joe and I were in a meeting two or three years ago, and somebody high up in the provincial leadership asked us what *reserve* meant. It really highlighted that they didn't understand what we were talking about. They thought that First Nations owned that reserve land. It's interesting to think of that across provincial leadership levels in the health system. They still don't understand some of the fundamental things that have, over generations, prohibited or created an impact on our ability to be self-determining. That's a good example of some of the conversations Joe was having with health system partners. We were trying to build partnerships, but at the same time helping them to understand the impact of settler colonialism and the continued impact that we see day to day.

"Joe approached these questions in such a good way that everyone would leave the room being like, *wow, Joe, thank you so much for helping me on my journey.* That is a role that he played in such a big way—helping other people on their own Journeys. Because everyone was at a different place and space."

Becoming hard-wired into the provincial health decision-making process was helped by Deputy Health Minister Stephen Brown's invitation to Joe to join his leadership council table. Brown wanted to see First Nations health become a common thread in strategic decision-making. At first, Joe was there only to discuss First Nations health issues, but soon it was clear that having him aboard as a full participant was valuable.

The BC Health Leadership Council met monthly to deal with issues in the health system, and the FNHA built a strategic policy team to align with health authorities to represent BC First Nations issues most effectively.

In my interviews with many individuals Joe worked with at all levels, I heard many stories about Joe's ability to be a great partner and help others become better partners, through his fair and tireless approach. The following stories speak volumes regarding what Joe accomplished by bringing people together, as well as the patience needed to succeed in the face of initial resistance.

Arlene Paton, BC assistant deputy minister, Population and Public Health: "The journey was so beautiful to watch. The first real memory I have of Joe is when we met with the First Nations Health Council. The Ministry of Health had agreed to start having some conversations not only with the ministry, but also the delivery arm of the health care system, which is the five Regional Health Authorities and the Provincial Health Services Authority. This was agreed to as part of the Tripartite First Nations Health Agreement.

"The CEOs of the health authorities and representatives of the First Nations Health Council therefore came together to meet for the first time as a group. Joe was there as the CEO, and I was invited through my role at the time in the Ministry of Aboriginal Relations and Reconciliation, and it was very tense.

We were at the Legislature, in a very formal room. The minister and deputy minister of health were there, the latter chairing, and there were the CEOs all lined up on one side of the table and the five First Nations Health Council representatives, plus Joe as the CEO, and I think his board chair was there and the ADM of Health, and me. It was like they were on different planets.

"The CEOs were saying: This isn't our problem. We don't have to deal with this. We don't even know why we're in the room having this conversation. And what do you mean the health system doesn't work for your people? It was difficult to watch.

I'm not sure what the CEOs had been told before the meeting, but they were not there in a constructive way. It felt as if they were hoping this would be a one-off and they could get out of there and go back to their real work. Joe, a couple of times, tried to lay out examples and opportunities to build bridges, because there can be very strong personalities on both sides. Representatives of the First Nations Health Council were becoming angry at what seemed to be stonewalling by the health care system. The deputy minister of health was chairing and trying to mediate and explain expectations.

"We had the Tripartite Agreement on First Nations Health, so these meetings were required to be convened every year, and sometimes twice or three times a year. When I moved over to the Ministry of Health in 2011 and became the ADM responsible for Population and Public Health, those meetings were still awkward, with a real sense of *them* and *us*. And it was a time for the political voices of First Nations to come in and rattle the senior executives of the health care system and get them to pay attention. The CEOs were kind of dismissive and not wanting to be there, but within a couple of years it was amazing how the partnership started coming together.

"I credit Joe for going out and meeting individually with each CEO to talk at the operational level, without the politicians, and to get to know them on a personal level. Joe encouraged and supported the CEOs in developing relationships with the chiefs in their regions. Some of the partnerships that grew out of this, between the local chiefs and their Regional Health Authority executive teams, started to make great strides. In fact, years later, the CEO of Interior Health was honoured by being blanketed by all 55 of the chiefs in that region when he retired. It was an incredible ceremony, where this tough-as-nails, finance-and-business kind of guy said to me after that it was the most moving and meaningful recognition that he had ever received in his career.

"Joe was able to help him and others in charge of delivering health services to understand the gap that we had. He was able to share real-life experiences of what was happening and what was not working for First Nations and be heard. For example, it shouldn't happen that someone is just discharged out of a hospital with no plan for how to access follow-up care if they're in a remote community or similar circumstances. Joe could bring partnership ideas forward because he also had resources and a role as CEO of the First Nations Health Authority.

"At the last five or six of the Tripartite meetings that I attended with the CEOs, the First Nations Health Council , Joe and the deputy, they were no longer lined up on opposite sides of the table. CEOs and First Nations leaders sat together to talk about how to keep improving the system for First Nations. They started problem-solving together. That journey was so beautiful to watch, because there was so much at stake.

"New investments were made, redirecting resources from within regional health authority budgets, because data demonstrated that the system had spent far less on this population that had lower health outcomes. That's part of Joe's leadership, that kind of bridge-building. He can be very, very firm, but he can also take the high emotion out of the room through his story-telling and his insistent "you actually need to listen to this" kind of approach. Joe was able to let the politicians be angry, but he was businesslike and able to present hard facts that were convincing and important.

"Joe's total commitment to have the First Nations Health Authority become an organization that walks the talk of being a First Nations organization was trailblazing. He insisted on a high percentage of First Nations hiring, through HR policies and training approaches. Leading with culture, he insisted that ceremony have a place in the day-to-day operations of the authority, with Elders providing advice and leadership. He was comfortable with the idea that the FNHA doesn't have to look or act like a Western organization.

"This is a repeatable model for First Nations healthcare for other provinces to look at. The BC health care system has this unique partner that can help bridge the service gaps, the patient journey, the cultural gaps, as well as ensure that First Nations' solutions to improve health outcomes are articulated in a way that the system can implement them in partnership with FNHA and with FN communities.

"Over the course of my career, I met with many of the chiefs of BC's 203 First Nations. A chief of a community, with 80 members or thousands of members, is responsible for all the municipal, provincial and federal authorities. It's often the chief and council and a small staff running the community's social services, health care, child and family development, housing, resource and economic development, drinking water systems, everything. If a chief was meeting with the minister of health, they might have an issue with, for example, access to ophthalmologists. The granularity of that issue would not be something the minister could respond to, but ministry staff could be directed to engage with the FNHA, the Regional Health Authority and the community and work out how best to serve that particular community. The public just has no idea how complicated these issues can become, or how hard it may be for some First Nations patients to navigate the system, let alone feel comfortable and respected within it.

"Joe's insistence on a focus on cultural safety and humility as a policy that everyone in the health care system needed to be trained in is having a long-term impact on BC's health care system. Each health authority now has a huge focus on cultural safety and humility. Do you as a health care worker or staff person know who the First Nations in your region are? Have you ever visited them? Do you know what their language is? When a First Nations person walks in the door, can you greet them and make them feel comfortable so that hopefully they won't walk out the door without getting necessary services?

"The cultural differences have been so often misinterpreted. Joe has been wonderful at making sure it was front and centre. He challenged the CEOs and the board chairs of the health authorities that they needed to be responsible for their staff to be culturally aware, culturally sensitive, and not to be discriminatory.

"Joe has dedicated his entire working career to lifting up First Nations. He's used his gifts to articulate and persuade and operationalize. I don't know how to put it, but he possesses a kind of persistence without being annoying. He would come back again and again, bringing more data and more evidence, until it's just so obvious what needs to happen that the barriers fall away. His authenticity plays a big part in this. I've watched Joe and the deputy minister of health have a conversation where Joe's been able to share ideas through personal experience and culture in ways that have really shifted the discussion. He's very down-to-earth. He really believes in what he's doing; he's been a wonderful leader and spokesperson for First Nations health."

Ian Potter was also in attendance in that initial meeting with Joe and the Health Authority CEOs. He, too, recalls it being a very contentious meeting. The BC minister of health, leading the meeting, was talking about everyone being onside. Then one of the health authority CEOs stated that he didn't know why he was there. First Nations are a federal responsibility, and even if we do treat First Nations, we treat them like anyone else. He basically described the meeting as a waste of time. This was, in many ways, the underlying understanding of the health authorities at that time.

Joe responded in a way that, according to Ian Potter, went something like this:

"Do you want every encounter to be safe?"

"Well, of course."

"And wouldn't you want equitable outcomes?"

"Yeah."

"Okay, we need to talk about how to get that, because it is not happening now. You may not think you are doing anything wrong, but these guys are always losing. Why is that?"

Ian Potter added, "That's where the document regarding cultural safety and humility was introduced to them, with ideas of what organizations could think about and what actions they could take to tackle systemic racism."

There was a lot of work to be done.

Lisa Lapointe, BC chief coroner: "Joe has such a clear way of articulating what needs to happen. As a First Nations person who grew up in a First Nations community, he has the cultural and worldview lens that non–First Nations people don't have. He pushes, but he pushes in a respectful way. He keeps pushing, pushing, pushing, with a dogged determination. He challenges you to think more openly, which is an amazing skill."

Cynthia Johansen, CEO and registrar, BC College of Nurses and Midwives: "One of the analogies I like to use to describe Joe's approach is the idea of pulling a sweater apart. He doesn't just grab one thread. Joe's secret sauce is that he looks at the sweater and then starts pulling on the different threads to see which one(s) are going to successfully unravel the whole thing. If a few of them get stuck, then he works on another. He's not prone to a fight-or-flight approach. He is programmed to look forward."

Perry Kendall, former provincial health officer: "It was quite amazing. I would go to board meetings over a number of years with the First Nations Health Authority, the federal and provincial representatives and the representatives from the health authorities. You could see the change over the years as people actually got to respect each other's positions, know where they were coming from, and start to trust one another."

44. Continuing to push the limits of Health Governance

2012 -The Health Partnership Accord

Joe: *Almost as soon as the Framework Agreement was signed and being implemented, we started finding that through the health governance partnerships being developed, the parties were already imagining transformational arrangements that would push beyond the limitations of this initial legal agreement. In the early days, both governments were uneasy and unsure of what a health governance partnership with First Nations would mean, but as it was nurtured, new and exciting possibilities for the benefit of all became apparent. Productive discussions with Canada and BC at that highest political level required the parties to capture their future interests in a political agreement to enable new possibilities that were beyond what had been contemplated so far.*

John: Certain challenges arose that needed a refreshed political understanding to act on the emerging opportunities. Joe spoke to the council about needing to reinvigorate the relationship with senior government officials, to give them permission to imagine more, to colour outside the lines of the legal agreements. That was the notion behind the Health Partnership Accord—an aspirational agreement looking above and beyond what was in the framework.

An excerpt from the Accord document: "Through this Health Partnership Accord, we commit to continue to work together to improve the health status of First Nations in British Columbia and to build a better, more responsive, and more integrated health system that will benefit all British Columbians. We make a commitment to take action in order to work together towards a future where BC First Nations people and communities are among the healthiest in the world. This

Accord sets out the principles and approach by which we will nurture our broad and enduring partnership and envisions the possibilities for our future success in health systems transformation."

The province was finding more ways to fund the FNHA, because doing things with and through the organization as partners was better than trying to figure it out for themselves. The provincial apparatus has its own limitations as to how things operate in its own institutions; numerous ways for leaders to tie themselves in knots. Working with the FNHA allowed for innovation. It was agile in comparison to the slow-moving provincial system. The Health Partnership Accord gave everyone permission to think beyond.

45. The History of Makara

Joe: *Sadly, we are often too busy in our work trying to build a better future for our people that we don't make the time to see our family. Makara was my newborn niece, and I never had a chance to hold her. She passed away after only a short eight weeks of life, before I was able to make my way home to meet her. Makara's death was a tragic and traumatic event for my family, but the interaction with the colonial system around her and my family was even worse. This kind of unfortunate situation happens far too often for First Nations people and served to reinforce my drive to address the racism and culturally unsafe interactions we have with government systems.*

John: Joe and I have shared many emotional discussions, but none were as emotional for Joe as when we talked about Makara.

On June 20, 2012, two-month-old Makara died suddenly, without warning. Makara was the youngest of five children, living with her family in Tla'amin. Makara had fallen asleep beside her mother and a sibling and never woke up. The cause of death was Sudden Infant Death Syndrome (SIDS).

An obviously tragic story on its own was made more difficult for the family by the coroner's lack of awareness or empathy for First Nations laws. Joe, as the uncle, had to stand his ground just to get the coroner to speak with him directly. They only wanted to speak with Joe's brother, the girl's father, which was not the way of the Tla'amin people where the family appoints a spokesperson for the family during periods of grief.

Once that was sorted, and they had determined that there was no criminal wrongdoing, Joe learned from the local coroner that Makara's body would not be returned intact within the time needed to fulfill Tla'amin death protocols. And her brainstem would be retained for additional testing, without the family's knowledge or consent.

While the coroner delivered all the wrong messages, Joe does acknowledge that he was just the messenger, and it was difficult for him.

Leveraging the support of many voices of senior officials in the Ministry of Health working on the First Nations health file, Joe reached out to BC's chief coroner and eventually managed to get the Coroners Service to agree to an exception for Makara's remains, which was good. But he still had to deal with the messages delivered by the Coroners Service, which shamed Joe and his family by saying, "Okay, we've agreed to give your niece back, but we need you to know that this is against the greater good of society." This was at the direction of public servants in Victoria and following protocol that called for the pathologist to retain eyes and brainstems in the case of SIDS. Joe challenged the concept of "a greater good of society," questioning how a white man could determine the action they were taking was for the greater good without any understanding of First Nations custom. He took on getting the coroner's protocol changed.

Joe didn't think the local coroner was aware at the time of the role he held with the First Nations Health Authority, but he did tell the coroner he was going to fix this for everyone. Following many meetings Joe and others had with the BC Coroner's Office, the Powell River coroner came back with his final report and told Joe there were many good things happening. The Coroners Service was working with the First Nations Health Authority, and it was just great. It wasn't clear whether he ever figured out that Joe had had a direct influence on that.

The impetus for Joe to push for what is now known as cultural safety and humility started with his niece's passing and their dealings with the Coroners Service.

In the end, he developed a strong relationship with the BC chief coroner. While the Coroners Service is not technically part of the health care system in British Columbia, for First Nations a holistic view of health and wellness encompasses death and spirituality.

The chief coroner recognized that the work they were doing was causing harm. Here is her recollection.

Lisa Lapointe, BC chief coroner: "I came back from lunch and there were numerous phone messages about the death of a First Nations infant in Powell River, and a number of concerns. What it boiled down to was that our coroner, in following investigative protocol, had let the family know that the infant's organs may be retained for further examination. At that time, the protocol at BC Children's Hospital was that they retained the eyes and brains of infants in a sudden infant death situation. Joe was one of the people phoning and I learned that he was the uncle of the infant who had passed away unexpectedly. Later I learned that Joe was the CEO of the brand-new First Nations Health Authority. That was my first introduction to the FNHA. I hadn't heard anything of it.

"We were able to resolve that situation on a one-off basis, where the pathologist agreed not to retain the organs and we were able to return the child to her family, Joe's brother and his wife, whole. This was necessary as part of the laws of their First Nation, and is common, I've learned with many First Nations, so that the child could pass to the spirit world intact.

"Joe opened a door for me that I hadn't even realized was closed, in terms of understanding First Nations cultural laws and beliefs and some of the very important tenets of the individual First Nations as well as some that applied more broadly. I learned that if a person can't pass through to the spirit world when they are supposed to, the doors to the spirit world remain open and other people may go before their time. I learned that newborns have a special role as an angel that will go to the spirit world to help the ancestors who have gone before them. To do this, they need to be sent to the spirit world intact, to do the work they are intended to do. It was really, really important that we understood the cultural laws and that we respected them for the sake of the health and wellness of the family and the community. We just had no idea.

So, Joe being Joe, he understood that, while it was resolved for his family, this must be happening for many First Nations families. In fact, it was happening for all families in the province, and that is one thing that Joe has always emphasized. We might make a change for the betterment of First Nations families, but in doing so we often change things for the better for everybody. So, we had a meeting at our office in Burnaby and a number of people at the table, including Coroners Service staff, a BC Children's Hospital pathologist and FNHA representatives, including Joe and Dr. Evan Adams. Grand Chief Doug Kelly was also present. It was a very open, frank and sometimes difficult conversation about our practice and why it had to be like that.

"It was a little bit heated at times, but what I've learned about Joe is, he's very insistent. He does not give up, and he is always very modulated in his approach. Joe doesn't show it, but I could sense his exasperation. At one point we were saying, based on what we were told by the pathologist, that it was necessary to retain the organs so that they could rule out any other disease and it was important for future learning, etc. Joe asked, "Well, when you do this, what do you learn? Show us what your studies have shown," and frankly, we didn't have that information. It was an embarrassing question. We had been doing this practice because that's what the pathologists advised was best practice. But we had never done any aggregate review of what was learned and whether it was beneficial.

"We ended up doing that review and found that there was virtually no benefit to routine organ retention, and we were causing harm to every family who was not getting their child back intact after their traumatic loss. Losing your infant child unexpectedly—healthy one day and gone the next day. We stopped that practice, and then there was a very long and tortured road for us and Joe, working collaboratively, to try to change the practice provincially. Eventually, after several years of discussion and support from senior health leaders, we established a Memorandum of Understanding with BC Children's Hospital that significantly restricted the occasions in which organs were retained. Ultimately, we developed a Post Mortem Diagnostic Service (PMDS) within the BC Coroners Service. The PMDS has dedicated forensic pathologists who conduct culturally safe, timely and geographically accessible autopsies to assist coroner's investigations. Culturally safe autopsies are a critical component of the Coroners Service commitment to culturally safe services."

Makara's legacy has been to transform a harmful practice into an opportunity to build new and respectful partnerships with BC First Nations people.

The Coroner's Office changed their practices in dealing with decisions about autopsies in the case of infant death. If it was determined that if there was no criminal wrongdoing, then the decision would go back to the family. This applied to all families—not just First Nations. Over a four-year period, extended investigations went from being performed 100 percent of the time to less than 10 percent. This allowed families to follow their death protocols and spiritual activities, so as not to trample further the mental health and wellness issues of the family already grieving.

Joe described the chief coroner to others in the health system as his best health and wellness partner—which would always get some funny looks. She is a champion for the recognition and importance of cultural safety and humility. She honours the right to self-determination for First Nations families. The FNHA supported the training of new coroners in keeping with that.

This initial effort was a catalyst for Joe's focus on "cultural safety and humility," which led to the signing of many declarations.

Signing ceremony with Lisa Lapointe, BC Chief Coroner.
Declaration of Commitment to Cultural Safety and Humility

46. Cultural Safety and Humility

Joe: *"Cultural safety and humility" was the beginning of the conversation to address Indigenous-specific racism in the health system. This principle requires the system and those who work in it to open their minds to another way of thinking. Listening more closely to what someone else has to say, so you have an opportunity to treat them as they want to be treated. In the early stages of this dialogue, the health system began to hear about the many harms the system caused to First Nations people. Diving deeper in the conversation, we start to understand that Indigenous-specific racism has been at the centre of how the health system interacted with First Nations people. To move forward we need to understand the origins of Indigenous-specific racism in our history of settler colonialism, and that this continues to shape our society today in a manner that privileges whiteness and continues to purposely oppress and harm First Nations peoples.*

BC Health Workers Cultural Safety Workshop

Deputy Minister for Ministry of Health and Addictions Doug Hughes signing Declaration of Commitment to Cultural Safety and Humility

John: Many organizations in British Columbia are open to acknowledging the traditional lands of the First Nations people at the start of gatherings, but this action carries little value if immediately afterwards they just return to their colonial ways. These acknowledgments are not like the national anthem before a hockey game. They are truths to be carried through whatever activity is being done.

We need to stop trying to fit First Nations' ways into our colonial systems. We've seen it attempted in hospitals, social services, policing, criminal justice, museums, and more. It's not working. We need real change.

Instead of trying to make First Nations fit, we must tear down our old thinking and build from there. That is Truth and Reconciliation. We need to be willing and open to listening to and understanding the truth before we move forward. It isn't sufficient to add a "token Indian" to a board or committee and say you have that box checked off. We need to support those First Nations individuals that are ready to take on those roles, and we need to support the development of new First Nations leaders.

From the start, the FNHA's approach under Joe's leadership included focusing on systemic racism and stereotyping that has led to culturally unsafe care and often real harm. *Cultural safety* was the term used until 2020 because the system was not yet ready for a conversation on racism. It has always been about racism, but racism was not called out directly until the 2020 "In Plain Sight" report.

The theme of cultural safety and humility was the cornerstone of what made the FNHA more than just a health organization run by First Nations. It made it an organization that could produce positive change through a First Nations lens. It challenged people to create a culturally safe environment and to understand that whether someone feels safe is a matter of *their* point of view, not yours. Without cultural safety and humility, First Nations could not get the benefit of the much larger provincial system, because it didn't work for them.

The health partners have all acknowledged that they should provide services to First Nations people at a certain level of quality based on cultural safety and humility. This builds trust, knowing they can get care when they need it, from early intervention onward. Many First Nations people, like Joe's dad, Norman, are reluctant to seek help until they are really sick. People need to feel safe using the system, to escape a long history of lacking early detection of treatable diseases.

Joe promoted the slogan of cultural safety and humility as he worked at helping the system understand the challenges First Nations people faced in health care, but its applications go far beyond that field.

2016 – Canada signs off on UN Declaration of Indigenous Rights

Canada finally became a signatory to the United Nations Declaration on the Rights of Indigenous Peoples (UNDRIP) in 2016. Article 8 of UNDRIP states that, "Indigenous peoples and individuals have the right not to be subjected to forced assimilation or destruction of their culture." And Article 12 adds: "Indigenous peoples have ... the right to repatriation of their human remains." Beyond the moral argument of Makara's story, the law is also now on their side.

Lisa Lapointe: "Joe represented the First Nations Health Authority, and more broadly, First Nations people, and then, more broadly, all cultures, so it really started a good conversation.

I didn't realize how ignorant I was, to be perfectly honest. I thought I understood settler colonialism. I think, on an intellectual level, I understood the level of some of the injustices, but until I got to know Joe, and was involved in meetings with him, and read items and books he recommended to me, I didn't get it. He opened my eyes to the impact and injustice. It's systemic racism, but unconscious over so many years, and it still exists in government.

The provincial government has adopted the principles of UNDRIP [United Nations Declaration on the Rights of Indigenous Peoples] in the BC Declaration on the Rights of Indigenous Peoples Act. Ministries are working to ensure their legislation and policy is consistent with the Declaration Act. It's key that this work is done in consultation with Indigenous peoples. Too often, committees are formed to ensure cultural safety for Indigenous people, without engaging Indigenous people. While the intentions are good, non-Indigenous people can never be looking through the same lens an Indigenous person brings."

Declarations of commitment to cultural safety and humility were signed by the BC Coroners Service as well as the FNHA's health system partners, including the provincial health authorities, the BC Ministry of Health, the health regulators, and the health professional associations.

These declarations provide a common vision, language, and framework that guides health system transformation, addresses systemic racism, and promotes culturally safe services.

Cultural safety and humility was brought up in most, if not all, discussions I had regarding Joe's work. In the spirit of listening to what others have to say, here are some of the responses I received in my discussions.

Harmony Johnson, consultant, former VP First Nations Health Authority: Cultural safety is an outcome, rather than an act, where someone feels that they have been treated safely and their identity is not just about not being discriminated against. It's about feeling that your identity is affirmed. It's not just this neutral thing of, "I treat you just like everybody else." I don't want to be treated like everyone else. I want to be treated like a Tla'amin person. I think cultural safety is an outcome that is only defined by me. Did I feel culturally safe in that experience? Everybody's experience is different.

"In First Nations health care, this means having our rights to decision-making upheld. We are involved in decisions on governance. Our perspectives are supported and included in processes of strategic planning of health authorities, or policy development, for example. We have our right to practice our traditions. In hospitals, they would have rooms available where people can do spiritual practice, or there's opportunity to do brushing or smudging or whatever.

"The fact stands, though, that institutions and society are built on colonialism, and colonialism was about expropriating land and territory from First Nations people. Racism greased the skids for settler colonialism, and so, while things have changed, so much of today's beliefs that the state has used to expropriate land and territory from First Nations people are still underlying all the ways we think about First Nations people. Like the belief in genetic inferiority that was used early on in history to say, well, they're sick. They're all dying. Let's just contain them on a reserve over there, and then eventually they'll die. That belief still exists. It's a common stereotype in health care that First Nations peoples are just genetically a little bit different.

"Humility is the fuel for all of it. The conversation about white supremacy is a whole other terminology that it puts people off. But the fact that we see white people as the top of that racial pyramid is reality. And so, there is a lot of privilege that comes along with that. The humility to be able to say 'I have something to learn, and I am not the expert in everything' is the fuel to then open your mind to involving First Nations in governance, to adapting your facilities to acknowledge their practice, and to not see those practices as inferior to your own.

"It's being aware that you have biases and to actively work to engage in every conversation with curiosity and learning, but also to really understand and probe into what it means to have an anti-racist approach.

"Cultural safety and humility is a broad, encompassing approach, where humility is the quality. Making room for our own beliefs and worldviews and then making space for our governance, our rights to govern and self-determination."

Mary Campling, former CFO, First Nations Health Authority: [Cultural safety and humility] is about how you want to be treated and how would you want your family member to be treated in a situation. It's a well-known fact that anybody with lower socio-economic status has poor health outcomes, regardless of race, nationality or anything else. When you add race to it, it becomes worse. The whole issue is of how people who are stigmatized, even when they go to someone they need help from, are dismissed because of who they are. If they are not treated with cultural safety and humility, they are likely to avoid care.

"English may not be their native language. I don't think most of us have any appreciation for the trauma that the residential schools produced, and how families were torn apart. We were never brought up with any of that knowledge, so we are extremely ignorant, and now I think a lot of people are afraid to ask questions because they don't want to show their ignorance.

"I only worked there for just over two years. I have to say, it's the most fortunate thing I have been able to do in my entire career."

*   *   *

Katie Skelton, FNHA, Anishinaabe, Ojibwe; member of Henvey Inlet First Nation:

Our partnership with Providence Healthcare is a good example of how we worked on organizational commitments to cultural safety and humility. In addition to providing primary care and residential care through a number of BC-based hospitals, Providence is responsible for the operation of St. Paul's Hospital, located in downtown Vancouver. An important part of their history is that Providence as an organization is linked to St. Paul's Indian Residential School, which was located in North Vancouver. The work that Joe did with our Elder Leonard George to set up that partnership was something that I'll never forget.

"It wasn't as easy as signing a declaration and saying, hey, we're going to work together. We couldn't do that without acknowledging the harm that their organization had caused for hundreds of First Nations people in British Columbia. They were ready and willing to talk about Truth and Reconciliation Commission Calls to Action and how their organization was going to uphold those calls, but it was Joe's leadership saying, well, we need to acknowledge the past. It was his ability to say that, as a leader of this organization, I can't make that decision on behalf of everybody. He worked with Leonard George and his son Gabriel George and really thought through the path of acknowledging that past, and having that leadership team understand what it meant. Doing it in a way that was culturally safe. It involved ceremony. It involved a feast. And then we could partner. We didn't go straight into partnering, because we knew that there was this work that had to be done.

"We were taking away this lens of saying, 'You have checked a box to be culturally competent,' to explaining, 'You've now taken a course in cultural safety, and it's a lifelong process.' Even as a First Nations person, I'm never going to be culturally competent. That shift of language has been a journey in and of itself, taking a health system away from competencies they are used to and saying that we want to create a space that's culturally safe. And the only people who are going to be able to say that the system is culturally safe are First Nations people who are experiencing that interaction in the health system. We want you to approach that space with humility. That's a big ask, because a lot of health professionals think that, well, I'm humble, I can do this—but then they need to recognize they have this systemic racism and bias that can peek its head up in different areas."

Cynthia Johansen, CEO and registrar, BC College of Nurses and Midwives: "In our roles as health profession regulators, we are helping to shape the system. We can't direct it, and we don't lead it. But in the way that we regulate the health professionals within it, we can shape and influence the system. We started working on the language for the declaration, and it took a long time. Not so much with the FNHA, but with my peers. We spent a lot of time dissecting every word and its potential impact on our organizations, rather than on the system and culture of health profession regulation. We got a bit stuck, looking at it from the perspective of: What will be our liability if we don't meet the outcome of the commitments? A very colonial perspective.

"We had to free ourselves of our mental model. It took a few months to get there, but it was worth the journey. I'm really proud of the declaration, because it is a foundational document. It's what we go back to when we are at a loss for how to move something forward."

Receiving a gift from Cynthia Johansen, CEO and Registrar of BC College of Nurses and Midwives, right, and Heidi Oetter, CEO and Registrar for the College of Physicians and Surgeons of BC, left.

47. Showing the Skeptics

John: It would have been a daunting task to create an organization with the scope and depth of the FNHA in any environment. Having the project led by First Nations and built for First Nations by First Nations meant the team faced no shortage of non-believers in the years leading up to the launch of the FNHA.

The Consensus Document that led to the signing of the Framework Agreement called for the FNHA and the health governance partnership to undergo an independent review every five years. The first evaluation was performed by an external management consulting firm in 2018.[45]

There was a tremendous amount at stake for the organization, with many believing that this major step in self-determination would fail. Despite the skeptics, and the extent of the leap being taken, the report acknowledged the first five years of the FNHA as a real success.

Critical to enabling the FNHA was the solid foundation being built in the form of the health governance partnership, which made it possible to expand the First Nations organization beyond the Framework Agreement—moves such as appointing its own chief medical officer. Success depended on the strength of the partnership with the province and federal government.

Of course, the report also identified some growing pains, specifically identifying, for example, a future risk of becoming too bureaucratic.

"The FNHA," the report stated in a rebuff to skeptics, "has become a successful example of a First Nations Organization that can deliver effective health and wellness services and respond to emerging needs." A repeatable model for other First Nations initiatives in self-determination.

The audit report went on to state other examples of its success:

---

45   https://www.fnha.ca/Documents/FNHA-Evaluation-Report.pdf

"The Parties achieved successful completion of transfer of responsibility for all activities formerly performed by the FNIHB–BC Region, including headquarters functions, to the FNHA, with many lessons learned to inform others across the country. The significant complexities and challenges of the transition period were addressed through the commitment and openness of partners, disciplined negotiations processes, established tripartite success factors, dedicated funding and robust briefing/communications/engagement processes. "

"The First Nations health governance structure, along with partnerships between BC First Nations and federal and provincial governments, has demonstrated reciprocal accountability and facilitated collaboration."

"The strength of partnerships, the establishment of Regional Partnership Accords, and a commitment by all partners towards cultural safety and humility has led to hardwiring the First Nations Perspective on Health and Wellness into the BC health system. The First Nations Perspective on Health and Wellness is permeating throughout the system."

"The First Nations health governance structure is generating value through new investment."

"There are early signals on improvement of health outcomes; however, more progress is needed."

"The FNHA has achieved significant progress in implementing important changes to First Nations health care in BC by advancing excellence in programs and services, championing the BC First Nations perspective on health and wellness, enhancing First Nations health governance, and operating as an efficient and effective First Nations health organization."

The report recognized the critical close partnership with the provincial government. It praised the recruiting of a First Nations chief medical officer, improved nursing services, bringing services closer to communities, and providing increased services to First Nations people living in urban areas.

"Transformative change takes time. The FNHA is still a young organization that has grown very rapidly while servicing a group that has been underserved since colonialization. It is dealing with competing priorities, emerging needs and resource constraints, so it will continue to experience some bumps along the way. There is always a risk in an institution the size of the FNHA that it could become bureaucratic, so it is important it never loses track of its original vision."

48. Wellness-focused

Joe: *Wellness is a fundamental component to the holistic world view of First Nations peoples. To be well, to live well, to be our best, is a strength-based philosophy/teaching that our people have held for thousands of years. Each of us are responsible and own our own health and wellness journey. Wellness is about the whole person being well and a catalyst for taking care of the care providers as well as those needing support on their health and wellness journeys. It is fundamental in the vision of the First Nations health and wellness organization the FNHA is supposed to be. It was something that would set the FNHA apart from Western colonial health authorities, who focus on treating the sickness of patients and may look to do more on the upstream prevention side but are unable to change directions. It is also an essential element when we look to benefit from the best of both worlds by incorporating traditional knowledge, teachings, and medicine with the best of Western medicine to support our people to live their best lives.*

John: One area where the FNHA was pushing for inclusion was a move to get everyone connected to a family doctor, while the province was driving to boost the number of physicians. At the same time, it wanted to ensure that when people did get connected, they received culturally safe care.

Issues addressed at the FNHA were not new, nor were they simple. It was a journey, not a matter of working from a checklist where something could be declared complete. The organization had become more visible, but not yet visible enough. People in the system were more aware of the need for cultural safety and humility, but there was still a long way to go. Too many people were not yet receiving the level of care that they should.

First Nations today have a big hole to dig out of. They are a long way from celebrating equal treatment, but at times simply making others aware there is an issue is an improvement. Many of the stories below may not seem like wins on the surface, but major strides are being taken.

Wildfires

The handling of wildfire issues in BC over the past few years is a good illustration of the importance of Premier Campbell declaring BC First Nations people as British Columbians. Without this, First Nations were considered a federal responsibility and were left on their own.

Evacuations were a major issue. Communities were being evacuated and then turned away from the evacuation centre because they weren't identified on the list of communities in the area to be evacuated. They weren't even visible. Even though the ancestors of these First Nations communities had lived in the area for thousands of years, the name of the community might be unknown to volunteers. In many situations, the community name had been changed to a First Nations name, which the intake people were unfamiliar with.

These evacuations were also triggering to people already traumatized by the fire. A particularly difficult example came about in the evacuation centre in Kamloops, where they were trying to shelter First Nations elders and community members in the arena. The responders were trying to provide support, but their ignorance was actually contributing further harm.

All the bunk beds were lined up just like they had been in residential schools, triggering painful memories in the survivors, on top of the stress they were already experiencing. That this was culturally unsafe was not understood by people unaware of colonial history and its impact on First Nations people. The evacuees didn't want to stay there. Understanding and accommodating their needs should have been part of the response, part of the playbook.

Joe formed a relationship with BC's deputy minister for Emergency Management, working on building better processes, understandings, and relationships. Getting everyone to work together and establish better ways of responding to emergency situations. He argued that planning for fires, pandemics and other emergencies should no longer be done in isolation from or exclude First Nations communities. Cultural safety and humility was needed at evacuation centres.

The Red Cross and other response partners all began to work more closely with First Nations communities, and the overall response improved. They were encouraged to work proactively around preparation and prevention initiatives, such as sharing heat maps of where they thought the fires would start and move, so they could get out in front and connect with communities in advance of a crisis.

The FNHA team on the ground served as a trusted source, helping to navigate and advocate for those communities. The FNHA had to develop capacity and support to implement emergency protocols, find accommodation, and provide food—all of which was well beyond what the organization had originally contemplated.

Allegations of Deep-Rooted Racism in Emergency Rooms

In a formal review in 2020, deep-rooted racism was found to be common in emergency rooms in BC. This was no surprise to anyone in the First Nations community. The "In Plain Sight" included 24 recommended actions for government and health care leaders. The many references to cultural safety and humility in this report are testament to the impact of Joe's work.

I spoke with Cynthia Johansen, registrar and CEO of the BC College of Nursing Professionals, after the findings became public.

"Ten years ago, I would have reacted differently to this situation, thinking: *Oh no, we are going to get so many complaints*. I have a very different view today. Our role is to help to correct this type of issue in the system. You can't correct a problem if you don't know it exists. As painful as it is to face these realities, it is through the discovery of the facts that we can understand better what is happening and then step into the space and make corrections. I think people are always scared that it's going to result in something punitive, and that may very well be the case in this situation. That is important, but in some respects secondary to the opportunity to fix the system for the longer term and make it safer for everyone in the future. Hopefully, we can take corrective action and then move forward with less harm.

"Most humans on the planet generally come from a place of trying to do the right thing, but sometimes we get caught up in unintentional bad behaviour and need someone there to call us on it. So, building that concept of a just culture where people, again, are humble enough to admit they have been doing things wrong, or in a way that is inappropriate, and then getting to a space where they can shift their thinking and behavior … that, to me, is a gift."

The "In Plain Sight" report included a specific recommendation that reflects Johansen's approach.

Recommendation 11

That the B.C. government continue efforts to strengthen employee "speak-up" culture throughout the entire health care system, so employees can identify and disclose information relating to Indigenous-specific racism or any other matter, by applying the Public Interest Disclosure Act (PIDA) *to employees throughout the health care sector without further delay.*

You can't fix a problem until you can identify its existence.

49. Crabs in a Bucket

Joe: *Settler colonialism deliberately caused harm to First Nations peoples for the purpose of getting rid of the "Indian problem." The intention was that First Nations people, with rights and title, would no longer exist. Over 150 years of Indigenous-specific racism, expressed through genocidal legislation, policies, practices, and narratives, has been effective in causing great harm and the oppression of First Nations peoples for the benefit of white society. It has effectively created divisions among First Nations people through the imposed Indian band structures and weakened our societies and our relationships. Strong First Nations leadership is needed to make a difference moving forward; however, progress is going to be difficult as we need to overcome the learned behaviours imposed by Western systems that fail our peoples and often pit our leaders against one another for various reasons.*

In 1967, Chief Dan George, chief of the Tsleil-Waututh Nation and award-winning actor, singer, and author, silenced the crowd of 32,000 people in Empire Stadium that had gathered to celebrate Canada's Centennial. For First Nations, Canada's 100th birthday was not something to celebrate, as George made clear. He spoke of their loss of freedom, their way of life, and their pride. He spoke of not forgetting the past, and also of building a new future. Of shattering barriers.

He spoke of First Nations rising up in government and industry and bringing their authentic selves to that.

"A Lament for Confederation"

"How long have I known you, Oh Canada? A hundred years? Yes, a hundred years. And many, many *seelanum* more. And today, when you celebrate your hundred years, Oh Canada, I am sad for all the Indian people throughout the land.

"For I have known you when your forests were mine; when they gave me my meat and my clothing. I have known you in your streams and rivers, where your fish flashed and danced in the sun, where the waters said, 'Come, come and eat of my abundance.' I have known you in the freedom of the winds. And my spirit, like the winds, once roamed your good lands.

But in the long hundred years since the white man came, I have seen my freedom disappear like the salmon going mysteriously out to sea. The white man's strange customs, which I could not understand, pressed down upon me until I could no longer breathe.

"When I fought to protect my land and my home, I was called a savage. When I neither understood nor welcomed his way of life, I was called lazy. When I tried to rule my people, I was stripped of my authority.

"My nation was ignored in your history textbooks—they were little more important in the history of Canada than the buffalo that ranged the plains. I was ridiculed in your plays and motion pictures, and when I drank your fire-water, I got drunk—very, very drunk. And I forgot.

"Oh Canada, how can I celebrate with you this centenary, this hundred years? Shall I thank you for the reserves that are left to me of my beautiful forests? For the canned fish of my rivers? For the loss of my pride and authority, even among my own people? For the lack of my will to fight back? No! I must forget what's past and gone.

"Oh God in heaven! Give me back the courage of the olden chiefs. Let me wrestle with my surroundings. Let me again, as in the days of old, dominate my environment. Let me humbly accept this new culture and through it rise up and go on.

"Oh God! Like the thunderbird of old I shall rise again out of the sea; I shall grab the instruments of the white man's success—his education, his skills—and with these new tools I shall build my race into the proudest segment of your society. Before I follow the great chiefs who have gone before us, Oh Canada, I shall see these things come to pass.

"I shall see our young braves and our chiefs sitting in the houses of law and government, ruling and being ruled by the knowledge and freedoms of our great land. So shall we shatter the barriers of our isolation. So shall the next hundred years be the greatest in the proud history of our tribes and nations."

The vision of building a new future and shattering barriers was something of which Chief Dan George spoke, and he was able to witness the early stages of progress in his lifetime. He passed away in 1981, as Joe and others like him continued the path he set out, by getting the "white man's" education and gathering skills.

When Joe went to university in 1979, he was one of few at that time from Tla'amin to have done so. Betty Wilson had gone before him and was supporting Joe in her role as education coordinator for the Tla'amin Community.

Evan Adams, former FNHA health officer, had also grown up in Tla'amin. He was a few years younger than Joe and looked up to him when he learned he was going to university. It was a time when many others from Tla'amin got serious about studying and becoming academics. A positive step in the direction Chief Dan George was fostering that also came with its own challenges.

To be successful First Nations leaders, they needed to fight for their rights as First Nations people, but also to fight against self-doubt, and all too often against their own people.

They had heard all their lives: *You can't have that, don't ever expect to be in that role, it's not for you.*

Evan talked about these low expectations: "In a way, most of us didn't think we would ever be used to our fullest potential. We could do our best, but it wasn't our game. We were getting ready for the game, but was anyone really going to play us? Indians can't win. Indians weren't seen as getting medals."

Working hard was not the issue. In fact, it was at the heart of his dad's and Joe's dad's teachings. "You get up, you work hard. Your body is meant to work hard. We were taught to push harder than we knew we could. That was just our way. That hard work has led to a significant number of people from the Tla'amin community playing prominent roles today."

Joe speaks of the Indian Act legislating First Nations people to administer their own poverty. They went from being a self-sufficient community that worked together, being their best selves, to fighting for limited resources as wards of the government. Individual success, or even the slightest possibility of it, was often regarded with suspicion.

As Evan describes it: "We were leaders, and because we came from a small community, we were also related. This would create trouble for us as we ran into each other in leadership roles. People would literally call us the 'Sliammon mafia.'"

They needed to survive their own people just to get a seat across the table from non–First Nations people.

In her book, *Caste: The Origins of Our Discontents*, Isabel Wilkerson discusses the historic and existing caste system in the US, its rigid structure, the direct influence it had on policies in Nazi Germany, and its similarities to the caste system in India. There might be some question as to the scale of the caste system in Canada compared to the US, but in terms of First Nations, the term certainly applies.

Wilkerson suggests that, "the greatest threat to a caste system is not lower-caste failure, which in a caste system is expected and perhaps even counted on, but lower-caste success, which is not."

The caste system "puts the richest and most powerful people of the dominant caste in the penthouse of an allegorical high-rise, and everyone else is in descending order on the floors beneath." Over generations, people learn where they belong in this societal structure. In Wilkerson's metaphorical tower, people in the lowest caste— in Canada, Indigenous people—are in the basement, which is at risk of flooding. First Nations were put in the basement by settlers who treated them as less than human.

Those in the higher castes, even just one floor up, will hold the bottom layer down even if it costs them something to do so. They won't accept the bottom layer becoming equal, even if they themselves would be better off. In the US, as an example, many low-income white people have voted against joining unions that would lead to higher pay and benefits, because they won't accept being treated equally with blacks. In Canada, it is our lowest caste—Indigenous people—who are held down by all groups that consider themselves higher up in the system.

Making matters worse, those in the lowest caste will often try to hold their own caste back. If someone in the lowest caste gets ahead, those at the bottom level feel their success only pushes them down further.

This is often referred to as "crab mentality." The story Joe shared with me goes like this: "An Indian fisherman was sitting with another guy catching crab. As he caught them, he put them in an open bucket, while the other guy put his crabs in a bucket but also covered them with a lid. He asked, "Why don't you put a lid over your crabs? Aren't you worried about them getting away?" The Indian fisherman responded, "No, I don't need to worry about it. They are Indian crabs. If one gets too high in the bucket, the others will pull him down."

First Nations not only face an uphill battle against multigenerational harms, systemic racism and white privilege, but the system put in place by the privileged class has evolved in such a way that they have become their own oppressors.

Evan spoke of challenges faced at the FNHA as people came into the organization who were related or personally acquainted and had those connections used against them. "Despite protocols being followed, there were people that were simply too jaded to accept this*f*. Good, talented, formidable people ended up being pushed out of key roles by those who were more interested in politics and power than in seeing amazing accomplishments. Despite all that Joe's achieved, he was not an exception to this rule."

Strong First Nations leaders are needed to achieve Chief Dan George's goals, yet some of them have ended up sitting on the bench.

"Our self-oppression, including our poor treatment of women, has held us back," Evan added. "It is systemic. These are not our teachings. Our teachings are to hold each other up. To be our best. We must encourage and support our next generation of First Nations leaders."

50. Leadership "Responsibility"

Leaving the team in a better place

Joe: *Leadership shouldn't be about power. It should be about responsibility. We are responsible to do our best, to leave the work in a better place than where it was when we started, for all of our First Nations peoples we have the honour to serve. We need to show up as our authentic First Nations selves and to also develop future leaders to take on the work. Finally, we need to know when to get out of their way when it's their time to lead.*

John: Numerous First Nations leaders have led through political activism. Joe's leadership has come through patience, perseverance, and in boardrooms. He has built teams by asking for help with things he wasn't good at. No one is good at everything. You need to know your blind spots and your weaknesses and proactively address them through leadership and the expertise of others.

Joe has helped develop a talented group of next-generation leaders, and I've been lucky to meet a number of them. We need to continue to support and provide opportunities to develop more First Nations leaders who lead in the authentic way Joe does.

He recognizes the need to provide opportunity for growth by First Nations people and at those institutions. He has helped First Nations leaders from the FNHA take on board of directors roles with the College of Nurses and Midwives and the College of Pharmacists. These are big roles, where a sole First Nations person is joining a board that has led systems in a certain way for years. Joe's support for the new board members and for educating non–First Nations board members has been very important. It's challenging to counter heavily entrenched ways of thinking and acting.

Harmony Johnson, former VP Policy, Planning, and Quality, FNHA: "Joe has a firm view in his mind about his own integrity and arranges his behaviour around that and expects others to do the same. He has a clear moral compass that he follows. He has high standards, and people are highly motivated to please him and do their best to meet these standards. He believes in partnerships, and nurtures partnerships to get systemic work done. He is committed to developing BC First Nations leadership."

Allison Twiss, former regional advisor, FNHA: "Joe had a way of inviting you into the canoe and to pull with him on the journey, as an ever-nimble navigator. He never lost sight of the star directing our course. Always with the vision of healthy, self-determining, and vibrant BC First Nations children, families, and communities in heart and mind, and quick to make adjustments as our journey unfolded. Always tweaking course to ensure the most efficient, safe, and best routes were taken, always adapting as needed, given smooth or rough waters. Never being fixed, and always staying true to the goal or the mission.

"Joe brought people into the work not just to be partners but as champions of the work, alongside him. He not only trusted in you, even as a junior staff member, but he also counted on you."

Janene Erickson, FNHA, grew up in Vancouver instead of her community of Nak'azdli Whut'en in Northern BC. She did not receive the teachings growing up that would have helped her to know her own identity. She became "part of a lost generation."

If not for becoming part of the FNHA under Joe's leadership, Janene believes she might have been assimilated without really finding out who she was. She credits that leadership, and being part of doing the related governance work, as directing her path to finding out who she is and giving her the confidence to lead. "I wouldn't be able to confidently be in a governance position or leadership role if I didn't get grounded and get that development and guidance from Joe, and

Knowledge Keepers Leonard George, Seqwalia [Ann Whonnock] and Sulksun [Shane Point] at the FNHA.

Katie Skelton, FNHA, Anishinaabe, Ojibwe; member of Henvey Inlet First Nation. Katie moved from her home in Ontario to join the FNHA. She is also a member of the board of the College of Pharmacists of British Columbia. Katie has her own story of how she has grown as part of the FNHA and been able, for the first time, to talk about her lived experience and be assured that her experiences as a First Nations person are valid. "Really understanding that our voice, our story, our experiences are real, and they matter. We didn't grow up with a lot of the tools or the culture that would make us succeed in leadership positions. The journey that we've been on, that Joe has been helping us with, has been to find our strength and root it down through our relationships, our partnerships, and our culture, and use that to gain strength.

"We were able to gain, through Joe's leadership and through Seqwalia and Sulksun, constant grounding and reaffirming that helped build us to a point where we could push back and provide positive input. Our experiences are unique, but at the same time so similar to First Nations all across the country, especially here in British Columbia. Our experiences are our strength.

"Joe would talk to us and remind us that we needed to do health first, because healthy people can go on to have healthy families. You see other areas across the globe creating economic development opportunities as the priority, and that's fine, but what was so unique under Joe's leadership was the acknowledgement that you need healthy people to make healthy choices. We are doing it for the hundred and fifty thousand First Nations people in British Columbia. We're doing it for seven generations to come. This reminded us to ground ourselves in that decision-making framework and acknowledge the importance of health. Healthy people can do amazing things."

51. Leaving the FNHA

Joe: *The work to implement the First Nations Health Governance partnership with BC and Canada is bigger than any one individual. It was an honour to be the inaugural CEO of the FNHA and have the opportunity to be involved, build, and implement the work for 14 years. There always comes a time when you need to move on, for whatever the reason. When the time comes, you want to be able to look yourself in the mirror and know you did your best. You should be able to look your people in the eye, and they will tell you if they think you did your best. I am proud of the work I did at the FNHA. There were many amazing people from all sides that I met as part of the work, who have enriched my life forever. It was good work and an honour to do my best for all First Nations peoples served by the FNHA.*

John: Joe doesn't want to ever be in a position where he has to compromise his values and ethics to get something done. He wants never to need a job that badly. Whether it was as CEO of the FNHA or as chief negotiator, he always wanted his integrity and values to define his work.

Joe approaches whatever he is doing with integrity, getting what needs to be done, done. He would not be compromised based on fear that his family or the band were going to say things. Since he first left home to go to UVic, he had tried to maintain control of his own life even within the highly politicized world he lived in.

He had seen too many people become compromised when they worked within the dysfunctional Indian Act system set up in First Nations communities. Situations that would take everything from you and then spit you out in the end. He didn't want to become dependent on his job to the point that he would start doing the wrong things just to hold on to a position.

He left the FNHA in October 2019, proud of the work that had been accomplished and happy to have stayed true to his vision and values while he was there.

Now that he has adjusted to the reality that he is no longer officially part of the FNHA, he looks back with tremendous pride. The institution is the first of its kind, and there are still strong partnerships there he is proud to have been involved in building. There is still a seat at the table for First Nations health leadership.

He is proud that he helped establish and lead an organization run by BC First Nations people for BC First Nations, and proud of the First Nations leaders that developed their skills at the FNHA. He is proud of working with strong First Nations women in key roles.

Sulksun, Knowledge Keeper, Coast Salish: As a leader in the FNHA, "Joe was the only person in BC doing anything for the 150,000 First Nations People in BC and the 203 communities speaking 20 different languages. I met the Dalai Lama. Joe is like him. He is one of a kind. A champion. Unwavering. One with Vision."

Part 11

NEXT

52. Qoqoq

Joe: *Qoqoq Consulting honours/holds the spirit of the White Owl. The medicine of Qoqoq is about opening our eyes. To see beyond the ordinary. To find a path through the darkness of confusion, misunderstanding, and shadows. It is about wisdom, intuitive knowledge, and being able to see with clarity beyond fear and illusion.*

John: Following his time at the FNHA, Joe re-established his consulting practice under the name Qoqoq (Qoqoq.ca), providing executive leadership support. For Indigenous institutions and organizations, he provides support in areas including Governance Development, Community Development, Strategic Planning, Organization Design/Development, Leadership Development, and Negotiations. For non-Indigenous organizations, he provides support in the areas of Social Justice and Racial Inequity, Cultural Safety and Humility, and Indigenous Partnership Development. His company has been in high demand from the start.

The name *Qoqoq* is a great fit. In Tla'amin, this word translates to "White Owl."

Elsie Paul, a Tla'amin Elder, shares a story where there was a healer who was helping a man who was not well. The man had lost his spirit from grieving the loss of his son, and without recovering it he would soon die. After proper preparations were carried out, it was Qoqoq, the White Owl, acting as a messenger between the spirit world and the living world, who brought back the grieving man's spirit, which returned to him his energy and his life.

Joe's reputation and skills also recently led to him taking on the role of vice president of Indigenous Health and Cultural Safety at the BC Provincial Health Services Authority (PHSA). He is doing this while also retaining consulting clients.

He accepted the role at the PHSA because of its province-wide scope and the importance of having First Nations people in executive leadership roles. He sees it as an important opportunity to deal with Indigenous-specific racism and to promote the concept of cultural safety and humility throughout the provincial healthcare system, and he sees First Nations executive leaders as the catalyst for the next great transformation in relation to social justice and progress for First Nations peoples.

Joe is also a volunteer board member with a couple of well-known organizations that are doing important work and are looking for guidance in support of First Nations/Indigenous issues. He is a dedicated, busy man who is still committed to answer the call for First Nations peoples.

53. John – Final Words

I started this journey ignorant of First Nations at best, and at worst, I bought into many common stereotypes. I had a simplistic understanding of racism and little understanding of what Joe had faced in his life. I didn't comprehend my white privilege.

Joe has been an unwavering and patient teacher. He has dedicated his life to First Nations rights and is not shy about expressing his beliefs. Like that old cough syrup commercial that said, "It tastes bad, but it works," Joe delivers truths that may be painful for some to accept, but we all need to hear them with an open mind. It is good for us.

Through the journey, I have gained a high respect for core First Nations values. I have learned of First Nations practices of consensus-based leadership, sustainability, and decision-making that looks seven generations forward and seven generations back. Do I believe these are the answers to all our problems? No, but should we listen to these ideas and incorporate them into our worldview? Absolutely yes. Our approach today is not working. Just look at our failures on climate change. We are trying to solve issues using the same approach that created them.

My eyes have been opened to the multigenerational trauma First Nations people have suffered. It is no longer impersonal for me. Every morning, I wake up seeing headlines regarding First Nations people being treated as "less than." These stories were there before, but I simply didn't give them their due. I read them passively—as just another story. The over-incarceration of First Nations people. Another First Nations child dying in "protective" custody. Another young First Nations woman missing or killed. Racism at the Canadian Museum for Human Rights, racism at the Royal BC Museum, ongoing racism in the medical system, policing, banks. Basically, in colonial institutions. It is happening every day. It seems ridiculous in retrospect, but I didn't know how bad things were, despite all the evidence in front of me. Joe has provided me with insight and awareness into many of the issues First Nations people face daily.

I have learned to understand the resilience of a people that survived every attempt to get rid of them. There is so much we can learn from First Nations about spirituality, sharing, and sustainable practices. My relationship with Joe has developed to the point where we have an accountability to each other that requires the journey to continue.

Joe has followed in the footsteps of other First Nations leaders who have dedicated their lives to improving the treatment of their people by fighting for their inherent rights. He led a change that provides First Nations with a voice in their own health care. He has brought First Nations health care closer to the level of non–First Nations treatment in BC. In some cases, thanks to the focus on wellness, he has made it even better for First Nations. Putting the institution in place, however, doesn't remove the racists or the systemic racism from the institutions the First Nations work with. As those who fought for rights, reconciliation, and fairness ahead of him found, it is a painfully slow process at times.

Today, Joe has prominent leaders calling him to get his help making changes where incidents of racism have made national headlines, due to ongoing systemic racism in health care, government institutions and Crown corporations.

The emotion that goes into our discussions is deep. I find myself exhausted by the issues, and at the end of the day, I can hide in my white privileged world. The struggle never turns off for Joe. He lets people know that the change we are after is not a 9-to-5 change required only in the workplace. Joe has chosen not to be a politician in a political First Nations' environment. He keeps it up every day, all day. The need for his work is also incredibly unfair.

I see how difficult it is for First Nations to gain proactive support from the non–First Nations population. It doesn't happen until we have participated in rich and emotional personal discussions. I have had the good fortune on this journey to meet with strong, intelligent, generous First Nations people. While many are leaders today, they all come with stories of painful life experiences they have had to overcome.

Hopefully this book will help bring more people forward. We need to move beyond just intellectual understanding and start thinking emotionally. First Nations people have been treated as "less than" for too long. I am hopeful that Joe's work is part of the tipping point, where the general population will "get it" and change will happen more rapidly.

Joe has said to me a few times, "If I don't do it, who will?" His dedication to his people and fighting for equity prevents him from relaxing and getting away. The least we can do is help.

To make change happen requires participation by the power of the majority. The privileged. White power. Those without power can only lobby, protest, and disrupt. They require those with power to support the change.

White people will never have the expertise that a First Nations person has regarding their oppression. We can gain a greater understanding, but they are the experts. We need to give them equity to fix things for themselves. We need to divest from our Whiteness.

Our systems and institutions were built by white people for white people, and in those systems white people thrive. And white people get elevated to leadership positions by their peers hiring people like them.

As white people we continue to receive unearned advantages, in contrast to the unearned disadvantages imposed on First Nations. That is systemic, yet when we talk about issues of race, we conveniently don't talk about the race that has the power.

We non–First Nations people need to recognize that you can't spend 150 years pushing a group down and then one day just say, 'We won't do that anymore,' and expect to have equity. We first need to help reduce their burden. I don't know what the complete solution looks like, but we do need to break down what we have in place today and rebuild together.

"Humility is not thinking less of yourself, it is thinking of yourself less."— C.S. Lewis

I was asked recently: "Knowing what you know now, what would you have done differently in the past?"

I'm not sure about my young self. I like to think I would have been more available to Joe. I would have said less and listened more. He also would have needed to share more. I wouldn't have dressed as Tonto.

As teenagers, though, we lacked maturity. We weren't ready to be advocates or allies.

We needed leaders supporting the truth. A better education. This is one of the reasons I am talking about these issues now. We need new leaders to understand the issues and speak up.

I acknowledge that, throughout my career, I primarily hired people who looked and thought like me. People that I perceived as confident and charismatic, while the characteristics I really wanted were competence, humility, and integrity. I was fortunate enough to work with some very good people, but we could have been better. I would have worked proactively to hire more people that were different from me. I would have spoken up more. I certainly wouldn't have gotten caught up in my own world and lost touch with Joe.

Racism, thanks in large part to the Black Lives Matter movement, is getting attention right now. There has been some positive movement from governments, including legislation in BC to ensure all laws are consistent with the United Nations Declaration on Indigenous Peoples (UNDRIP). At the same time, we also have prominent Canadians saying we don't have a racism problem. We need to take every opportunity, while racism is being talked about, to educate others and take inventory of our own behaviors.

We can put away our default "white lens." This takes real intent, because it is deep within us.

We can listen and learn with humility. We can treat the First Nations community as "more than," to help them reach the point where they are no longer "less than." As longtime oppressors, we need to give something up, but we will gain so much more in return, in authenticity and in the power of relationships.

White privilege is like riding a bike with the wind always at your back. It's an advantage you don't recognize until you turn and ride the other way. It is our turn to reverse course and cut through the wind for the First Nations community. It's time to provide more support and give them a chance to achieve their goals. Once we get to that point, we can turn around again, and we can all ride with the wind at our backs.

I understand the importance of humility—of being open and teachable. I understand the need for truth and reconciliation. Of respecting First Nations territories, beliefs, Indigenous laws, cultures, and their way of life.

It is time to change the dialogue. I have had discussions with Joe and other First Nations people about what it means to be an ally. I am still learning, but my starting point is to speak up.

I do not know what it is like to stand in Joe's shoes, but I am very proud to stand beside him. I am committed to including my voice in the fight against racism and for reconciliation.

54. Joe – Final Words

This book focuses on a lot of my history, so I want to acknowledge some of the people that helped me see things the way I do today. My mom had an amazing level of integrity and courage, and she showed me what I needed to know to shape my own ethics and values. That's who she was, even with how bad things would be for her. She was always such a good person, and I miss her every day.

The greatest gift I got from Dad was his work ethic and conviction. He lived life on his own terms, the best that he could. He would fight for what he wanted; if he had something to say he said it, and when he wanted something done, he got it done. Dad did the best he could for his family in the only way he knew how at the time, based on the world around him. It was a tough journey for him, like it was for many of our people, but he never lost his focus. My dad was his own man, and I wish I could talk to him about the changes happening in our world today.

My parents were both survivors.

Growing up, I was just trying to be good. To be perfect for my dad. I have been able to translate that into just being the best I could be for myself. That's our job, to be the best we can for ourselves. I started seeing some of the challenges people were having in our community and could better recognize where people were coming from.

When I see people doing the best they can in a situation, whether they succeed or fail, I try to understand where they are coming from and where they are on their health and wellness journey. That kindness and level of acceptance is what I saw a lot of in Mom.

I also learned from the support of a few teachers in elementary school and high school and coaches over the years. Some genuinely good people like Hew'kin, Joe Mitchell.

Besides being my first soccer coach and a leader in the community, Joe was a generous man and a Knowledge Keeper for the Tla'amin people. He was one of my first mentors/teachers and had an easy way about him. He exhibited great knowledge and kindness. He demonstrated patience and taught through humour and storytelling. I was very fond of him.

Over the years I had other influences. Working at the Victoria Friendship Centre and getting to know Alex Nelson taught me a lot about real commitment to our people. He is a generous man and was always willing to take me in if I needed a safe place to hang for a while. I still stay in touch with him.

My time working with Qut-same, Leonard George, was a true gift. His ability to demonstrate great humility in leadership and his willingness and generosity to share his teachings and culture with me and the FNHA greatly influenced the type of leader that I strive to be. Today I continue to be fortunate to work with Sulksun, Shane Point. We have many great conversations, and his teachings and wisdom continue to ground me in a good way.

I also want to acknowledge my friend John, who has co-authored this book with me. I appreciate him reaching out to me after all those years and have been fortunate for our respective journeys to reconnect at this time of our lives. So much has had to happen in both of our lives for us to be willing to do this difficult work together. One of the biggest reflections for me is when John let me know that he had thought I wouldn't make the soccer team at UVic. The truth of that moment is so much like what my world was for most of my life. I knew I would have to learn to walk alone most times, if I was to be successful in the things I wanted to do. I do appreciate his honesty to be able to share that with me, as well as his worry for me not to be hurt. I believe this type of honesty is what is necessary for us to go on this journey together. From our time together we have rebuilt our friendship on different terms. John has demonstrated a willingness to learn and understand and is open to being in that uncomfortable space that his privilege has protected him from for all these years. We share a common belief that we need to leave the world in a better place for our children, and together we are doing what we can to make that a reality. John is a very determined individual when he puts his mind to something. His willingness to engage in conversations with other people of white privilege will be his greatest contribution to this effort. He can have conversations that I can't have, or shouldn't have, and even though they are difficult for him, he is prepared to engage. And finally, John has been focused on completing this project.

With his persistence were able to get this over the finish line. I have had many distractions from this project over the last year as I have embarked on a new chapter in my professional career. The full benefits of completing this book, for me on a personal level, are many and I would not have realized them without John's persistence. For that I will be forever grateful!

There are also many other people, far too many to name, who I have utmost respect for and who have a special place in my heart. They are family, friends, soccer coaches, teammates, opposing players, and work colleagues. Each of them has provided an opportunity to build a unique relationship and to help me understand the world around me. Relationships that were all meaningful and have helped me experience this world as a First Nations boy and then a man—to see how everything comes together, both good and bad.

There is a very generous spirit within the First Nations community that took time for me to understand, but once I did, I would pick up a lot of the good thoughts and feelings. The tricky part is acknowledging that as human beings we are not perfect, and with a lot of our folks, especially what they've gone through with residential school and all that, is trying to see the good in them and understanding. I understood that when I went back home after university. I eventually would leave again, but it was a matter of just trying to understand people and see the good in people, and then recognize the bad parts and put those into context.

Part of building our nations is about breaking the cycle of the harms that have been perpetuated. It is also about creating the opportunity to build a bridge to allow First Nations people to relate with Canadian society in a way that is culturally safe and respectful *of our rights. We want them to be able to cross that bridge without experiencing harm and without losing their identity. We want them to be able to come back and say, I did this with one group, and this with another. They should be able to live somewhere else for a while and still come back no less Tla'Amin than they were before.*

How does our generation do what it can to leave the world in a better place for our children and grandchildren? We are trying to make sure it's better than what it was. I feel I am working to provide that for my son. As a parent, I suppose you always feel you could have done more, but we do enjoy spending time together. I am, and always have been, very proud of him.

For me it has been a journey to understand the beauty of being from the First Nations world. I realized my life is not defined by the stereotypes, and that I don't have to go live on the reserve, be a drunk, fight with my wife or my kids, to be an "Indian." That is not what being First Nations is about. That was just the result of a colonial-designed societal structure intended to eliminate First Nations and other Indigenous peoples.

Being First Nations is so much more than that. We have a connection to the land, to our families and our ancestors. We are gifted with vision to guide us into the future and live our lives with strength derived from love, compassion, and generosity. We have responsibility and purpose and so much to offer the world around us.

When I reflect back on my life, for me, it was initially about survival. My path could very easily have veered a different way while I was growing up and determining my identity. Fortunately, there are many good people who are willing to share their gifts with you if you are looking for them. They have helped shape the route in life that I did take. I had to find my own space of self-determination and free myself from the societal construct intended to destroy the First Nations spirit within me. Each of the relationships I encountered with people became a choice for me.

The way Sulksun recently described it is that we need to know that we are all medicine, and that we get to choose whether we are good medicine or bad medicine for one another. When I am at my best, I choose to be good medicine and seek out others who are good medicine for me. Our First Nations teachings give us everything we need to be our best. Our Knowledge Keepers are always there to share the teachings with us, so the guidance is there.

A long time ago, it came clear to me that I no longer had to accept that others can determine where we as First Nations people would be situated in society. Although the racism continues, it is not mine, and I need to be strong and resilient to keep moving forward. My soccer identity first helped demonstrate this to me, and from there I have continued to strengthen my connection to our teachings and rich history to guide my leadership approach and how I live my life. Today, I am very clear that, not only are we moving into a time where First Nations are "Less Than, No More," but in reality, we never were, and now society is seeing us for the first time!

OTHER RELATED VOICES FROM HANCOCK HOUSE

The Best of Chief Dan George

Chief Dan George & Helmut Hirnschall

978-0-88839-544-3 [paperback]
978-0-88839-190-2 [epub]
5½ x 8½, sc, 128pp
$12.95

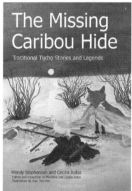

The Missing Caribou Hide: Traditional Tlicho Stories & Legends

Wendy Stephenson and Cecilia Judas

978-0-88839-762-1 [paperback]
978-0-88839-763-8 [epub]
8½ x 11, sc, 48pp
$12.95

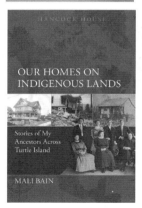

Our Homes on Indigenous Lands: Stories of my Ancestors Across Turtle Island

Bain, Mali

978-0-88839-741-6 [paperback]
978-0-88839-748-5 [epub]
5½ x 8½, sc, 202pp
$24.95

HANCOCK HOUSE PUBLISHERS LTD.

19313 Zero Avenue, Surrey, B.C. Canada V3Z 9R9

#104-4550 Birch Bay-Lynden Rd, Blaine, WA, U.S.A. 98230-9436

(800) 938-1114 Fax (800) 983-2262

www.hancockhouse.com info@hancockhouse.com